T0214176

ES6 for Humans

The Latest Standard of JavaScript: ES2015 and Beyond

Deepak Grover
Hanu Prateek Kunduru

Apress®

ES6 for Humans

Deepak Grover
Delhi, India

Hanu Prateek Kunduru
Seattle, Washington, USA

ISBN-13 (pbk): 978-1-4842-2622-3
DOI 10.1007/978-1-4842-2623-0

ISBN-13 (electronic): 978-1-4842-2623-0

Library of Congress Control Number: 2017944929

Cover image by Freepik (`www.freepik.com`)

Managing Director: Welmoed Spahr
Editorial Director: Todd Green
Acquisitions Editor: Louise Corrigan
Development Editor: James Markham
Technical Reviewer: Phil Nash
Coordinating Editor: Nancy Chen
Copy Editor: Karen Jameson
Artist: SPi Global

Distributed to the book trade worldwide by Springer Science+Business Media New York, 233 Spring Street, 6th Floor, New York, NY 10013. Phone 1-800-SPRINGER, fax (201) 348-4505, e-mail `orders-ny@springer-sbm.com`, or visit `www.springeronline.com`. Apress Media, LLC is a California LLC and the sole member (owner) is Springer Science + Business Media Finance Inc (SSBM Finance Inc). SSBM Finance Inc is a **Delaware** corporation.

For information on translations, please e-mail `rights@apress.com`, or visit `http://www.apress.com/rights-permissions`.

Apress titles may be purchased in bulk for academic, corporate, or promotional use. eBook versions and licenses are also available for most titles. For more information, reference our Print and eBook Bulk Sales web page at `http://www.apress.com/bulk-sales`.

Any source code or other supplementary material referenced by the author in this book is available to readers on GitHub via the book's product page, located at `www.apress.com/9781484226223`. For more detailed information, please visit `http://www.apress.com/source-code`.

Printed on acid-free paper

Dedicated to our parents.

Without them, we wouldn't be where we are today.

Contents at a Glance

Contents

About the Authors

Deepak Grover is a software architect from India, who has been helping several startups grow and build scalable products. He holds a Master's degree in Software Engineering and has been programming for the past eight years. He is proficient in JavaScript and has built several open sources libraries using ES6, ReactJS, and Angular 2 from the ground up. Besides computers, he likes to travel and can be often found speaking about JavaScript at tech meetups.

Hanu Kunduru is a computer languages polyglot and has worked extensively with C, C++, Java, Python, Ruby, and JavaScript. He is a serial entrepreneur with experience building and scaling technology and web products. Previously a CTO at a tech startup, he has experience managing large developer teams and workflows. He currently works as a staff member at 42 Silicon Valley in California, a coding school with a revolutionary project-based, peer-to-peer learning environment.

About the Technical Reviewer

Phil Nash is a developer evangelist for Twilio, serving developer communities in London and all over the world. He is a Ruby, JavaScript, and Swift developer, Google Developer Expert, blogger, speaker, and occasionally a brewer. He can be found hanging out at meetups and conferences, playing with new technologies and APIs, or writing open source code.

Acknowledgments

We would like to thank Louise Corrigan for scouting us and providing us with this amazing opportunity to share our love for JavaScript with the rest of the world.

This book would not have seen the light of day if it were not for the tireless efforts of the immensely supportive and responsive team at Apress. A very heartfelt thanks to Nancy Chen and James Markham for being extremely patient with us through deadline breaches and extensive rewrites.

Special thanks to Phil Nash, for his incredibly insightful and on-point reviews that immensely affected the end result of the content in this book.

We would like to thank all our friends and family who are too many to name individually, for motivating us and supporting us through this entire journey. Finally, we wanted to acknowledge the countless developers and contributors that are part of the JavaScript ecosystem, constantly innovating and pushing boundaries; you continue to inspire us.

CHAPTER 1

■ ■ ■

Getting Started with ES6

Around 46% of the world's population have Internet access today and the numbers are steadily increasing. While you're reading this, there are people out there who are using Internet services to book a cab, or a flight, or a table for two at a fancy restaurant; the point is that the Internet today has made people's lives easier. More and more web apps are being built everyday with the goals of saving people time, providing them with a higher standard of comfort or simply for entertainment. These apps are accessible on the go, and a lot of them are built using JavaScript.

According to the StackOverflow Developer Survey, JavaScript is the most commonly used programming language on earth. The ubiquity of the web platform is driving developers to use JavaScript more than any other language, leading to the evolution of JavaScript platforms like Node.js, front-end frameworks like Angular & React, and complete webstacks like MEAN (MongoDB, ExpressJS, AngularJS and NodeJS).

This book discusses the core concepts of ES 2015 (popularly referred to as ES6) and beyond, while focusing on the best development practices. By the time you finish reading this book, you will have a good understanding of core ES6 concepts, features, and their applicability in the modern-day development workflow.

ES6 The Specification

For many years ECMAScript 6 (ES6) had been in the works but on June 17, 2015, the 109th Ecma General Assembly approved the 6th Edition of ECMA-262 standards, making official a major upgrade to what we know and love as JavaScript.

The evolution of JavaScript, more specifically ECMAScript, is primarily community driven and TC39 is the official committee in charge of it. TC39 is primarily constituted by members that represent various stakeholders like the major browser companies and other invited members. They meet and communicate on a regular basis and are tasked with maintaining and upgrading the standard for the ECMAScript programming language and the libraries that extend its capabilities. In the process, they consider and evaluate the proposals for complementary and additional technologies for evolving ES. If you are interested in knowing more or checking out the agendas and minutes of their meetings, they are all available online on GitHub (https://github.com/tc39/tc39-notes).

The design process for ECMAScript standards is built around proposals that are usually popular requests from the developer community for new features or upgrades to existing ones. Since TC39 has a large number of participants, making it difficult to

© Deepak Grover and Hanu Kunduru 2017

D. Grover and H. P. Kunduru, *ES6 for Humans*, DOI 10.1007/978-1-4842-2623-0_1

do collaborative design work, usually one or two committee members are assigned as champions responsible for maintaining a proposal and to do design work and report back to the committee.

For a proposal to become a standard, it has to go through multiple stages. The initial feature sketch of the proposal, which is also referred to as a "Strawman proposal," is the first stage discussed by the committee and if it agrees that it is important, it is considered an official proposal. The proposed feature then needs to be implemented at least by two major JavaScript engines to get feedback from the community and evolve the proposal further. Once the proposal passes through these stages and incorporates feedback, TC39 approves it and will include it in the new edition of the ECMAScript standard.

History of ECMA, ECMAScript, and JavaScript

For someone unaware of the history of JavaScript, it can get pretty confusing quickly with so many different names like JavaScript, ECMAScript, different version numbers, and other popular offshoots like ActionScript, JScript, and TypeScript, which are all different forms of JavaScript.

JavaScript was originally developed by Brendan Eich as a scripting language for the web for use in the Netscape browsers. The name itself was chosen for marketing reasons due to the rising popularity of Java around the time, even though it had nothing to do with Java. In an attempt to standardize the language and the specification, it was submitted to ECMA International, a body for standardization of information and communication technology and consumer electronics. Eventually, the language standardized in ECMA-262 was just called ECMAScript or ES in abbreviated form, since JavaScript was a name trademarked by Sun and now belongs to Oracle. None the less, the language is still commonly referred to as JavaScript by everyone. There were many variations in implementations with ECMAScript as the backbone, like a slightly different adoption for the Internet Explorer by Microsoft called JScript. ActionScript is another example of a derived language developed by Adobe.

The initial versions ES1 and ES2 were released in 1997 and 1998, but in 1999, the ES3 release was a major upgrade with new features like regular expressions, improved string handling, more control statements, better error handling, and try catch exception handling among many other enhancements that we commonly use in JavaScript today. It had a widespread base implementation in various forms across major browsers and engines.

After the release of ES3, work on ES4 was well under way with many radical changes and a massive scope. Updated features included new syntax, modules, classes, classical inheritance, private object members, optional type annotations, and more. The proposed changes led to many differences, both technical and political, among various stakeholders in the community, resulting in it being put on hold in 2003. Parts of the proposed features made their way into implementations like ActionScript and Jscript. NET. After receiving feedback from these implementations, TC39 decided to resume work on ES4 in 2005, but by this time there was a big split in the community and two major groups had formed with differences on the way forward.

The alternate version championed by companies like Microsoft and Yahoo with fewer feature additions and improvements to the existing spec was referred to as ECMAScript 3.1. Because there was no consensus between the groups and the future of JavaScript was questionable, there was no major progress for a few years. Finally, in 2008 TC39 came to a consensus between ES4 and ES3.1. ECMAScript 3.1 was eventually standardized as the fifth edition of ECMA-262, also described as ECMAScript 5, and the committee never released an ECMAScript 4 standard to avoid confusion. ES5 would be a small incremental update and they would work on the next major release, which would be more modest than ES4, dropping many proposed features like packages, namespaces, and early binding. This proposed release was code named ES Harmony due to the nature of the meeting.

ES5 was released in December 2009, and it is currently the most widely supported version in modern browsers today. It came with many enhancements to the standard library and updated language semantics via a strict mode.

When it was apparent that plans for ES Harmony were becoming too ambitious for a single release, they split up the first set of features with the highest priority and code named the release ES. Next, to avoid premature naming with a version number in light of what happened with ES4, once it matured the specification was called ECMAScript 6.

ES6 took a long time to become official. The deadline for ES6 proposals was May 2011 and no major proposals were considered after that; but starting with the later versions, TC39 decided to time-box releases and release a new version every year with smaller incremental changes using whatever features are approved by that time. Hence the committee decided to change the naming convention of the versions to denote the year of release. Hence the official name of ES6 was changed to ECMAScript 2015 just before the final release, but the name ES6 was so widely used for years that ES2015 is still commonly referred to as ES6 and that's why we chose to refer to the new specification as ES6 throughout this book. But going forward, ES versions will be officially referred to by their year of release. So when we say ES6, we are referring to the broader changes in ES2015.

To look at ES6 from a bird's eye view, the specification drafts are divided into four major parts: the goals, the requirements, the means, and the themes. The goals aspire to fix the common pitfalls in JavaScript and add new features, while the requirements state that both of them need to be done in such a way that it does not break any existing code, while preserving the lightweight nature of the language.

We won't be digging into all the goals here. But you should know that these goals aspire to make it a better language for writing complex applications, libraries, etc. Keeping versioning simple and incremental, ES6 avoids versioning; this is best described by the philosophy of One JavaScript. For example, in ES6 everything is ES6 code: there are no parts that are specific only to ES5.

ES6 aims to provide better support for large applications and library creation. It offers enhancements like classes, modules, lexical block scoping, iterators, generators, native language support for promises, and much more.

The development of ECMAScript Standard is community driven and the requirements and features of the language will still continue to evolve for betterment in the future releases.

One JavaScript

In principle, when there is a new version of a language implementation, it is a chance to clean it up and remove old outdated features and make way for newer, better implementations. This leads to versioning, which basically implies that each piece of code needs to be linked to a specific version of the language. For example in Python, to shift between Python 2 and Python 3, one would need to migrate the code base. But this option would not be feasible for the web and a language like JavaScript. You will always have old chunks code that you will encounter on the Internet.

So the ES specification aspires to upgrade the language and avoid versioning. This is done by always being backward compatible, that is, all valid ES5 code is also valid for ES6 code. Therefore, ES6 is designed to not have any breaking changes and none of the previous features are removed. Hence in theory specifying the version is not required for the engines. So instead of removing existing features, you introduce new and better features.

What does this mean for you, a JavaScript developer? Since ES6 is a superset of ES5 you will not need to migrate any old code. Your existing JS code is valid ES6 code as well. Therefore to reiterate there is nothing you need to do. Therefore, everything you learned and use in existing JavaScript can be brought over to ES6, and it has more and better tools to add to your existing arsenal. This can be really helpful if you wish to incrementally port your current system into ES6 because everything is backward compatible.

Using ES6

Many JavaScript environments including web browsers and Node.js are actively working on implementing all the features of ECMAScript 6 and later. But it will take some time before ES6 is universally supported all across the Internet. At the time of writing this book, the latest version of chrome has 97% of features implemented and Safari has 100% of the features implemented. You can check the current feature-wise support for all engines at http://kangax.github.io/compat-table/es6/.

Until all of ES6 features are universally supported we need a way of converting ES6 into compatible JavaScript code. This is where transpiling comes in. Transpiling (transformation + compiling) is a technique in which we use special tools to transform ES6 code into its closest equivalent, ES5 code, to work on older browsers or environments.

Consider the following ES6 code:

```
const fruits = ["apples", "bananas", "oranges"];
let store = {
        fruits
};
store.fruits; // ["apples", "bananas", "oranges"]
```

This roughly transpiles to:

```
var fruits = ["apples", "bananas", "oranges"];
var store = {
        fruits: fruits
};

store.fruits; // ["apples", "bananas", "oranges"]
```

Some ES6 features can work simply by using polyfills or shims, which are simple patterns that define a new behavior in an older environment. You can also run and transpile small pieces of ES6 code online in your browser through ES6 REPLs like https://jsfiddle.net/ and babeljs.io/repl/. But for larger projects, you would need to use any of the available transpilers. We recommend using Babel, which is one of the most popular JavaScript transpilers available today.

Setting Up ES6 Using Babel and webpack

In order to use ES6 in your projects today, there are a set of build tools you will need to get things up and running. In this section, we will be discussing a few build tools, and we will be setting up an ES6 Boilerplate that you can use as a starter kit for your ES6 projects.

Transpiling with Babel

Babel.js is an awesome tool that lets you transpile your ES6 code into ES5 code that can then be run in current JavaScript environments. Babel supports the latest version of JavaScript through syntax transformers, and these plug-ins allow you to use new syntax, without waiting for browser support.

The first step is to install Babel on your local machine using npm.

■ **Note** Before you continue, make sure you have Node.js and npm already installed. If you don't have node and npm installed, you can visit https://nodejs.org/en/ to set up your development environment.

```
npm install -g babel-cli
```

Now, you can run any file with ES6 code from your command line using:

```
babel-node <filename.js>
```

But transpiling every file manually isn't efficient and, in most cases, isn't the solution for managing large projects. So let's set up an ES6 starter kit that will help you automate the build process and make the development process more efficient.

Setting Up an ES6 Boilerplate

In order to transpile an ES6 project, we will be using babel-loader and webpack that will help us generate a bundled output with all the transpiled code and related dependencies.

Start a New Project

Run the following set of commands in your terminal to start a new project:

```
mkdir es6-boilerplate
cd es6-boilerplate
npm init -yes
```

npm init creates a new project with its own package.json and –yes flag prevents npm from prompting you from any options and will use the defaults.

Install webpack and webpack-dev-server

Webpack is a very flexible module bundler that takes modules with dependencies and generates static assets representing those modules. We will be using webpack to let babel-loader transpile our ES6 code into traditional ES5 code and generate a bundled output file.

```
npm install --save-dev webpack
```

Besides webpack, we need to use webpack-dev-server to serve our app and transpile the code on the fly. But, note that webpack-dev-server is a development server and should not be used for production.

```
npm install --save-dev webpack-dev-server
```

■ **Note** To read more about webpack and webpack-dev-server in detail, you can visit https://webpack.js.org/concepts/.

Install Babel in the Project

You can install babel into your project very easily using the following npm packages:

```
npm install --save-dev babel-loader babel-core babel-preset-es2015
```

The next step is to configure babel to use ES2015 presets by adding a new file .babelrc in the root directory of your project with the following JSON:

```json
{
    "presets": ["es2015"]
}
```

Your package.json file should more or less look like this:

```json
{
  "name": "es6-boilerplate",
  "version": "1.0.0",
  "description": "ES6 Boilerplate",
  "devDependencies": {
    "babel-core": "^6.24.1",
    "babel-loader": "^6.4.1",
    "babel-preset-es2015": "^6.24.1",
    "webpack": "^2.4.1",
    "webpack-dev-server": "^2.4.2"
  }
}
```

Now, create a new index.html file and index.js file in the root directory of your project And your current project directory should look like the following:

```
├── index.html
├── node_modules
├── package.json
├── index.js
```

Configuring Webpack

The next step is to set up webpack by creating a configuration file - webpack.config.js in the root directory of your project.

A webpack configuration file is a CommonJS-style module where a configuration object is exported out of this module.

```
// webpack.config.js

module.exports = {
    entry: './index.js',
    output: {
        path: './dist',
        filename: 'bundle.js'
    }
};
```

Here, entry is the path to the source of your project and webpack will analyze your entry file for dependencies and generate a bundled output (which includes all the dependency modules). Note that only the entry module is executed on startup.

Add Loaders

Loaders allow you to preprocess files as you load them. Loaders provide a powerful way to handle front-end build steps and can transform files from a different language, like CoffeeScript to JavaScript or inline images as data URLs. For example, babel-loader uses Babel to load ES2015 files.

So now, modify webpack.config.js to process all .js files using babel-loader:

```
module.exports = {
    entry: './index.js',
    output: {
        path: __dirname + '/dist',
        publicPath: '/dist/',
        filename: 'bundle.js'
    },
```

```
module: {
    rules: [{
        test: /\.js$/,
        exclude: /node_modules/,
        use: 'babel-loader'
    }]
}
};
```

The above configuration implies the following:

1. './index.js' is the entry point of the application.

2. Output will be generated in './dist/bundle.js'.

3. We are processing every .js using the babel-loader, excluding node_modules to avoid external libraries to go through Babel, slowing down compilation.

Adding Your Generated bundle.js script to your index.html

Now we can include the bundle.js script into our html file to run the code.

```
<!DOCTYPE html>
<html>
<head>
    <meta charset="utf-8">
    <meta http-equiv="X-UA-Compatible" content="IE=edge">
    <title>ES6 Boilerplate</title>
</head>
<body>
    <h1>ES6 Boilerplate</h1>
    <p>Check console for details</p>
    <div id="main"></div>
    <script src="dist/bundle.js"></script>
</body>
</html>
```

To compile your .js file, you can run the following command in your terminal:

webpack

You can also use following additional flags with webpack:

- webpack for building once for development.

- webpack -p for building once for production (minification).

- webpack -w for continuous incremental build in development (fast!).

- webpack -d to include source maps.

■ **Pro Tip**   We can achieve prettier output using webpack – progress – colors that add a progress bar and colors in the webpack output in the terminal.

Setting Up a Development Server

To start a development server to test your code, you can run the following command:

```
webpack-dev-server -d --progress --colors
```

This binds a small node-express server on localhost:8080, which serves your static assets as well as the bundle (compiled automatically). It automatically updates the browser page when a bundle is recompiled.

We can also add these webpack commands to your package.json scripts.

```
"scripts": {
    "start": "webpack-dev-server --hot --inline",
    "watch": "webpack -w -d",
    "build": "webpack -p"
},
```

Now, you can use this:

- **npm start** to run a dev server at localhost:8080 and watch for/ recompile on changes.

- **npm run watch** to only watch for/recompile on changes on your own web-server.

- **npm run build** to generate a minified, production-ready build.

Let's try this out with a helloWorld() function inside our index.js file:

```
const helloWorld = () => {
    console.log("Hello! We are all set!");
    console.log("Arrow functions are working");
};

helloWorld();
```

To ensure everything is working perfectly, you can run npm start in your terminal and check the server running at http://localhost:8080.

You can run npm run watch to see the transpiled code in your bundle.js file located inside the dist directory, which will have this chunk of transpiled ES5 code:

```
function(module, exports) {
        "use strict";
        var helloWorld = function sayHello() {
            console.log("Hello! We are all set!");
            console.log("Arrow functions are working");
        };
        helloWorld();
}
```

Finally, we also recommend using ESLint in your project to use best practices and avoid errors while writing your code. You can find the above boilerplate code at https://github.com/metagrover/ES6-boilerplate, which also has an .eslintrc file that contains the standard rules and configurations we use.

Summary

JavaScript is one of the most powerful languages on the Web today, and it is only getting stronger. ES6, or officially ES2015 and the versions that follow, brings in a new paradigm to JavaScript. As we will see in the next few chapters, there is a lot of new stuff for a conventional JavaScript developer. But it is important for existing JavaScript developers to become aware of the new features to stay ahead of the curve as more and more features become mainstream in the world of browsers and frameworks.

JavaScript is moving quicker than ever before and transpilers and shims/polyfills are important tools to keep you on the forefront of where the language is headed. ECMAScript 6 comes with a very extensive list of new additions to the language and each of these features was carefully considered, discussed at length, and chosen by the community to become a part of the standard. Now it's up to us developers to use and apply the new standard to our products to better serve the people using them.

You might be asking yourself, is the change worth it. Is integrating ES6 into your projects and work necessary and do you really need to change the existing ways of doing things. We would like to say "Yes, it is worth it," and through this book we aspire to encourage you to adapt to this new world. Even if you face some resistance in moving away from the old ways, we suggest you stick with it and change your practices.

The JavaScript community is extremely vibrant and dynamic with things changing at a rapid rate. ES6/ES2015 knowledge is now expected among JavaScript developers. The new language constructs have not only become popular, but are now also widely supported. Mastering the inner workings of ES6 will let you build modern applications and give you access to a more powerful language and help you improve your programming skills.

Through ES6, you will have access to more powerful programming concepts like practical object oriented code among other new features that were simply not possible in the past. We hope to introduce you a modern workflow and tools like Babel and Webpack to make application development faster and more enjoyable. You will then be able to measure code quality and write more testable JavaScript.

CHAPTER 2

■ ■ ■

New Syntax in ES6

The new features introduced in ECMAScript 6 represent the foundation upon which JavaScript applications will be built in the future. In this chapter we will take a look at the changes and new additions to the ES6 syntax that help in fixing a lot of things that went wrong with the previous versions of JavaScript. We will discuss in detail about new ways of declaring variables and defining scope. We will also introduce new concepts like arrow functions, default function parameters, spread and rest operators, and object literal extensions.

Variable Declarations: let, const, and Block Scoping

In the past, all variables in JavaScript were declared using the keyword var. These variables were function scoped, meaning their scope was within the function enclosing them, and this could sometimes be confusing to developers coming from other languages. So, if you needed to create a new block with its own scope, you would have to wrap your desired code inside a regular function or an immediately invoked function expression.

Following is an example of regular function level scopes:

```
var price = 10; // Global Declaration

function showPrice() {
        var price = 12; // Local Declaration using var
        console.log(price); // 12
}
showPrice();
console.log(price); // 10
```

Following is an example of function level scopes with IIFE:

```
var price = 10; // Global Declaration
(function () {
        var price = 12; // Local Declaration using var
        console.log(price); // 12
})();
console.log(price); // 10
```

© Deepak Grover and Hanu Kunduru 2017
D. Grover and H. P. Kunduru, *ES6 for Humans*, DOI 10.1007/978-1-4842-2623-0_2

The above code demonstrates that the variable price is now scoped to the enclosing function and the changes are not leaked to the parent scope, in this case global scope. The new value price = 12 is only available inside the enclosing function scope.

If we replace the function scope with a block scope ('if' block), it looks like this:

```
var price = 10;
if (price) {
        price = 12;
        console.log(price); // 12
}
console.log(price); // 12
```

The above code makes it clear that the changes inside the 'if' block are leaked to the parent scope, which tells us that the var declarations are bound to the function scope and does not create block scopes.

Prior to ES6, JavaScript used functional scoping, but block scoping is more common than functional scoping across most programming languages. With ES6, we now have two additional ways for declaring variables, let and const, both of which declare variables that are block scoped.

Block Scoping with let and const

Quite simply, block scoping means that a new scope is created between a pair of { }. The variables declared using the keywords let and const only exist within the innermost block that surrounds them.

In the following example, what do you think will be printed to the console when you execute the following code snippet?

```
let nbr = 42;
{
        let nbr = 1000;
}
console.log(nbr);
```

The value 42 is printed to the console, because the second nbr variable is scoped to the block within which it is declared and does not affect the nbr variable outside of the block, where it remains 42. Normally, you wouldn't use a block like that unless it were in a control flow statement like an if condition or in a loop, but this explains how a variable is block scoped.

We now know that var is bound to function scope, whereas let and const are block scopes, which means if you've got a set of curly brackets (a block of code), you have a block scope. But, the catch is you can declare a variable inside of its block scope only once.

On the other hand, unlike let, const creates immutable variables. The values of the variables created using const need to be assigned during declaration and cannot be changed later in the program.

Consider the following example:

```
const value = 42;

console.log(value);    // 42
value = 1000;          // TypeError
```

■ **Note**   Trying to change the value of a const variable will throw a TypeError. Changing an immutable binding in strict mode only causes an exception SetMutableBinding().

Make sure that you always initialize the variable with a value declared using const; otherwise it will throw an error. Consider the following example:

```
const item;  // SyntaxError: Missing initializer in const declaration
```

If you need a constant with an undefined value, you'd still have to do something like this:

```
const value = undefined;
```

If you know that the value of your variables is not going to change throughout your code, you should be using const; otherwise use let to declare your variables. We recommend moving away from the practice of using var to declare variables as it is cleaner, more efficient, and easy to debug if you use block scoping. let and const avoid the source of misunderstanding, especially for programmers with expectations set by languages with block scope. let and const throw an exception if you try to access the variables declared by them outside the blocks they were declared and do away with *hoisting*, helping you localize the effects of your code fragments.

Consider the following example to understand how *hoisting* affects the variables declared using the keyword var:

```
console.log(nbr);  // undefined
var nbr = 42;
```

The above example prints undefined to the console because of hoisting. When we declare the variable nbr using var, due to hoisting it becomes equivalent to declaring the variable at the start of the scope with its value set to undefined. But if you moved the console.log statement after the declaration, it would print the number 42, due to the fact that entering the scope of the variable declared using var, that is, its surrounding function, creates a binding. The variable is then initialized by setting the value to undefined. When the execution reaches the declaration, this variable is then set to the specified value in the assignment statement.

Let's take a look at a similar example using let:

```
console.log(nbr); // Reference Error: nbr is not defined
let nbr = 42;
```

This would actually give you a *Reference Error: nbr is not defined* since no hoisting takes place here. This can be a big help in debugging different types of bugs that can be caused by a variable being used before it is declared. This Reference Error is technically called a **Temporal Dead Zone (TDZ)** error because you are accessing a variable that's been declared but not yet initialized.

More on Temporal Dead Zones

The main takeaway from this discussion is that let and const declare variables with a temporal dead zone (TDZ), in contrast to the hoisting that happens when you use var. The variable in the Temporal Dead Zone is not yet initialized with any value. A memory binding is created and remains uninitialized when the variable is declared. Trying to get or set the variable at this point raises a **Reference Error**. When the program flow reaches the declaration, the variable is then set to the value specified in the statement; otherwise it is set to undefined if there is no assignment in the statement.

const works in a similar fashion, the only difference being that it needs an initializing value during declaration, which cannot be changed later.

```
let data = true;

if (true) { // enter new scope, TDZ starts
    // Uninitialized binding for "data" is created

    console.log(data); // ReferenceError

    let data; // TDZ ends, "data" is initialized with "undefined"
}
console.log(data); // true
```

As soon as the initialization occurs with the assignment of a value to the variable, the TDZ ends.

The temporal dead zone primarily exists to catch errors. You should not be able to access a variable before it is declared, and even if you do by accident you should be warned about it. TDZ was the best solution for const to work the way it does and having let also having a TDZ makes switching between them very easy. TDZs helps us ensure that a variable in runtime always has the correct value.

```
if (true) {
    console.log(typeof anUndeclaredVariable); // 'undefined'
    console.log(typeof random); // ReferenceError (TDZ)

    let random;
}
```

Even if you try to access a variable in the temporal dead zone using typeof, you will get an exception. typeof is a safe way to check if a variable exists or not. But if a variable is declared using let further down in the code, it will throw a TDZ error because that variable is in the temporal dead zone when you call typeof. Therefore, it is a good practice to always make variable declarations at the top of your scope. This check is also useful for conditionally creating global variables using var. You can check if a global variable exists by doing something like this:

```
if (typeof globalVariable === 'undefined') {
    var globalVariable = { ··· };
}
```

■ **Note**   const is used to declare an immutable variable but it does not make the value contained in the variable immutable.

In the following code snippet obj is a constant, but the value it points to is mutable; therefore you can add a property to it but you cannot assign a different value to obj.

```
const obj = {};

obj.key ▪ 42;

console.log(obj.key); // 42

obj = {}; // TypeError
```

If you wanted to you could make the value itself immutable by freezing it.

```
const obj = Object.freeze({});

obj.key = 42;

console.log(obj);    // {}
```

Remember that Object.freeze() is shallow. It will only freeze the properties of the object passed to it. Only one level of properties of the object become immutable and not the objects that might be stored in its properties.

Variables Declarations in loops

For loops (for, for-in, for-of) let you declare variables in their heads. But the way you declare these variables using var, let, or const changes things. Let's look at each of these cases.

In a basic for-loop, using var creates a single binding for that variable

```
let arr = [];

for (var i=0; i < 3; i++) {
```

15

```
    arr.push(function () { return i });
}

let value = arr[0]();

console.log(value); // 3
```

You might have expected the output to be 0, but the output is 3 because a closure gets formed over the variable i at the end of the loop. i is set to 3 and each instance of i in the body refers to the same binding. Therefore, the function always returns 3. Now let's take a look at the case where i is declared using let:

```
let arr = [];

for (let i=0; i < 3; i++) {
    arr.push(function () { return i });
}

let value = arr[0]();

console.log(value); // 0
```

When we use let in a for-loop, each iteration of the loop will get its own i variable and any closures created close over their own value of i.

In the case of const, it works similar to var because the initial assigned value to a const variable will not change again.

```
for (const i=0; i<3; i++) {
    console.log(i);
}

// TypeError: Assignment to constant variable (due to i++)
```

Variable Declarations with Function Parameters and Global Scope

If you declare a variable using let inside a function, having the same name as a parameter, ES6 will throw a static (load-time) error.

```
function fn(param) {
    let param; // SyntaxError: Identifier 'param' has already been declared
}
```

Doing the same with a var does nothing, because it is just equivalent to re-declaring a variable. Another way of fixing this issue would be using a let inside a block, but the new variable declared will only shadow the parameter:

```
function fn(param) {
    {
        let param;
    }
}
```

The global object in JavaScript (*window* in browsers and global in Node.js) has always been confusing. That's why in ES6 a distinction was introduced. Consider the following example:

```
let notGlobal = "hello";
var isGlobal = "what up";

{ console.log(notGlobal); } // hello
{ console.log(isGlobal); } // what up

global.isGlobal //'what up'
global.notGlobal // undefined
```

All properties of the global objects are global variables. Therefore, in the global scope var declarations and function declarations create such properties. But global variables created using let and const declarations will not be properties of the global object.

Arrow Functions

Arrow Functions are another major syntax update in ES6. Arrow functions are functions defined using a new syntax, the "fat" arrow =>. The arrow is based on a similar concept from CoffeeScript. They help in making code more readable by opting out of the *function* and *return* syntax and read the same way the function executes. In this section, we will discuss in detail about how arrow functions are used and when it makes sense to use them.

The basic syntax of an arrow function is as follows:

```
var fn = data => data;
```

The first part of the left-hand side of the assignment statement is the argument that is provided to the function. If there is only one argument, you do not need any additional syntax. The next part is the arrow and then the expression that is to be returned. In this case it just returns the argument. The function is effectively equivalent to

```
var fn = function(data) {
    return data;
};
```

Consider another example:

```
let getNumber = () => 42;

console.log(typeof getNumber); // function
console.log(getNumber()); // 42
```

In the code above, we declare a new function called getNumber and assign it using an arrow function. The empty parentheses () denotes that the function has no parameters and finally, the function returns the value 42. In arrow functions, we can leave out the return keyword. The expression specified after the arrow will get returned *as long as it is not wrapped in { }.*

```
var getPrice = (quantity, tax) => (quantity * 5) * (1 + tax);
console.log(getPrice(2, .095)); // 10.95
```

Note that you can skip the parentheses () in case of exactly one parameter, but you will always need to use it when you have zero or more than one parameter.

If you want to specify a more traditional function block with more than one expression you need to wrap the body in braces. But you would specifically need to use the return keyword to specify the return value. Check the following code snippet for an example:

```
var getPrice = (quantity, tax) => {
let price = (quantity * 5)
price *= (1 + tax);
return price;
}

console.log(getPrice(2, .095)); // 10.95
```

Curly braces represent the function's body. If you want the arrow function to return an object literal outside the body, you must wrap the literal in parentheses. For example:

```
var getNumber = data => ({ data: "check", number: 42 });

// effectively equivalent to:

var getNumber = function(data) {
    return {
        data: "check",
        number: 42
    };
};
```

An object literal wrapped in parentheses shows that the braces are an object literal instead of the function body.

Using Arrow Functions to Create IIFEs

Functions in JavaScript can be used to create immediately invoked function expressions or IIFEs. You could define an anonymous function and call it without having any reference to it. This is an effective pattern to shield the expression from the rest of the program.

```
var fn = function(number) {
    return {
        getNumber: function() {
            return number;
        }
    };
}(42);

console.log(fn.getNumber());        // 42
```

In the code above, an IIFE is used to create the getNumber() method, which uses the number argument as a return value, ensuring the number property is effectively a private member of the returned object. Something very similar can be achieved using an arrow function as well by wrapping it in parentheses.

```
var fn = ((number) => {
    return {
        getNumber: function() {
            return number;
        }
    };
})(42);

console.log(fn.getNumber());        // 42
```

One distinction to note is that arrow functions are function expressions and are not function declarations. They are anonymous function expressions that have no named reference for the purposes of recursion or event binding or unbinding.

There's more to arrow functions than just the pretty and cleaner syntax. Arrow functions do save us a few lines of code and characters, but the real purpose of the arrow functions is to handle the this keyword within functions. this behaves differently inside an arrow function. But before we discuss that, in the next section let's take a look at how the this keyword works in general.

A Tale about this

In JavaScript, this is the current execution context of a function. Let's take a look at what it means in the following scenarios:

1. Function Invocation

Invocation of the getContext() function in Chrome will print the Window object in the console. That's because the context of the getContext() is Window/Global object. At the time getContext() is called, JavaScript automatically sets this as the global object, which in a browser is Window.

```
function getContext() {
    console.log(this); // Global or Window
}
```

When this is used outside any function scope, it also refers to the global scope. Check the following code snippet:

```
if (this === window) {
    console.log("this refers to the Global context");
}
```

■ **Note**   If you're in strict mode ("use strict"), this would be undefined.

---

2. Method Invocation

Method invocation means an object's method is called and in this case, this is the object that owns the method in a method invocation.

```
let myObj = {
    name: 'fancy',
    operation: function() {
        console.log(this);
    }
}
```

```
myObj.operation(); // { name: 'fancy', operation: [Function: operation]}
```

Method Invocation, that is, on calling myObj.operation(), [myObj object] will be printed in the console.

Now, let's try this:

```
let x = myObj.operation;
x(); // Window
```

Here, x refers to the operation() method inside [myObj object]. Calling x() would mean that we are making a function invocation instead of a method invocation and therefore, this will refer to the Global (or Window) object.

If we were to call x with the [myObj object] (for method invocation), we will have to use .call() method:

```
let x = myObj.operation;
x(); // Window
```

```
x.call(myObj); // { name: 'fancy', operation: [function]}
```

3. Constructor Invocation

Constructor invocation happens when an object is created using the new keyword. Consider the following example:

```
function Employee(name, department, salary) {
    this.name = name;
    this.department = department;
    this.salary = salary;

    console.log("Welcome " + this.name + "!");
}


let john = new Employee('John', 'Sales', 4000);
// Welcome John!
```

new Employee('John', 'Sales', 4000) is a constructor invocation of the Employee function. The result of execution is a new object and this refers to the newly created object.

The constructor function Employee() can be written as a class in ES6 that we will discuss later in this book.

this in Arrow Functions

Let's take a look at how this works inside an Arrow function. Arrow Functions are designed to lexically bind the context, which means that this refers to the enclosing context where the arrow function is defined. Unlike a normal function, an arrow function does not create its own execution context, but takes this from the outer function where it is defined. Consider the following code:

```
function Employee(firstName, department, salary) {
    this.firstName = firstName;
    this.department = department;
    this.salary = salary;

    this.getInfo = function() {
        // outer function context = Employee object
        return function () {
            // inner function context = Global object
            console.log(this.firstName + " from " +
    this.department + " earns " + this.salary);
        };
    }
}


let jim = new Employee('Jim', 'Finance', 5200);
```

In the above example, we created a constructor function called Employee and created a new employee object called jim using the constructor function with the new keyword. In order to print the employee information, we need to use the function returned by jim.getInfo(). Check the following code snippet:

```
let printInfo = jim.getInfo();
printInfo();  // undefined from undefined earns undefined
```

Here, printInfo refers to the inner function and since we are simply making a function invocation, this refers to the Global object that does not have any Employee properties and hence produces undefined whenever a property on this is used.

Let's look at how this behaves differently if we replace the inner function with an arrow function:

```
function Employee(firstName, department, salary) {
    this.firstName = firstName;
    this.department = department;
    this.salary = salary;

    this.getInfo = function() {
        // outer function context = Employee object
        return () => {
            // inner function context = surrounding context = Employee object
            console.log(this.firstName + " from " +
        this.department + " earns " + this.salary);
        };
    }
}

let jim = new Employee('Jim', 'Finance', 5200);

let printInfo = jim.getInfo();
printInfo();  // Jim from Finance earns 5200
```

In this case, the this keyword refers to the context of the function enclosing the arrow function unlike the previous case where it referred to the Global object. At this point, it is important to note that arrow functions do not change their context on invocation. Consider the following example:

```
function Employee() {
    this.firstName = 'Mike',
    this.department = 'HR',
    this.salary = 4500,

    this.getContext = () => {
        console.log(this);
    }
}
```

```
let mark = new Employee();
mark.getContext(); // [Employee object]

let context = mark.getContext;
context(); // [Employee object] (regardless of a function invocation)
```

In the above example, the context of the arrow function was set on declaration and it cannot be changed. An important thing to note here is that you cannot "rebind" an arrow function. The context is always fixed. Check the following code snippet for an example:

```
var details = {
        number: 42,
        operation: function () {
                return () => console.log(this.number);
        }
};

var details2 = {
        number: 84
};

details.operation().bind(details2)(); // 42
```

In the above example, we are setting the details2 number to 84. But we know we cannot bind a new object to the arrow function. The engine does not throw any error, it just ignores the bind completely. So 42 is printed even if we call the operation method with the details2 object. This also applies to call and apply. So with an arrow function, calls to **bind, call,** or **apply** will not be able to change to value of this.

It is clear from this example that inside a function the value of the this keyword cannot be changed. The value of this inside a function will remain constant, but you will still be able to use bind, call, and apply on arrow functions.

```
var product = (x, y) => x * y;

console.log(product.call(null, 2, 3));        // 6
console.log(product.apply(null, [2, 3]));     // 6

var multiply = product.bind(null, 2, 3);
console.log(multiply ());                     // 6
```

Apart from the lexical this, arrow functions also have lexical arguments. They don't have their own arguments array but instead inherit from their parent. There are no this, super, arguments, and new.target bindings for arrow functions, so the value of this, super, arguments, and new.target inside a function is the nearest containing non-arrow function.

23

■ **Note**   Normally in JavaScript extra newlines between code do not mean anything and the code still works properly, but with arrow functions, it is a problem. We cannot put the arrow symbol on a newline. ES6 forbids a line break between the parameter definition and the arrow of an arrow function.

Another important aspect of Arrow functions is that they cannot be called with new since they do not have the construct method and cannot be used as constructors. They will produce an error when used with new. Check the example below:

```
var newFn = () => {},
    object = new newFn();  // error - you can't use arrow functions with
'new'
```

Normally when a function is declared in ES5, it has a prototype property that is used in construction functions. But since you cannot use new on an arrow function, there is no need for a prototype. Hence, functions declared using arrow function, do not have access to a prototype field.

```
var details = () => 42;

console.log(details.hasOwnProperty("prototype")); // false
```

Similar to non-arrow functions that do not have duplicate named parameters in strict mode, arrow functions cannot have duplicate named parameters in either strict or non-strict mode.

Using Arrow Functions

So whenever you have a short single-statement inline function expression, with a computed return value and the function does not make a this reference a self-reference, you can replace it with an arrow function.

If you have functions that use the var self = this hack to deal with the this issue, or a .bind(this) call for proper this binding, arrow functions were built to help out with this exact problem. For example, consider the following code snippet where we are waiting for 1 second to toggle btn-active class on btn click.

```
$('.btn').on('click', function() {
        var self = this;

        setTimeout({
                $(self).toggleClass('btn-active');
        }, 1000);
});
```

Without arrow functions, we will need to store the context in a variable to be able to access it inside our setTimeout function. This can be simply rewritten with arrow functions as this:

```
$('.btn').on('click', function() {
        setTimeout(() => {
                $(this).toggleClass('btn-active');
        }, 1000);
});
```

Hence, along with shorter and more concise syntax, arrow functions handle the this keyword a little differently, making it easier to manage the code in many situations.

Default Function Parameters

Unlike the common pattern in other languages, functions in JavaScript are unique in the aspect that they allow you to call them by passing any number of parameters irrespective of the parameters declared in the function definition. This gives the developer an opportunity to use any value for the parameters in case no argument is specified. In ES5, if the argument is not specified, its value would be set to undefined. The pattern commonly used to set defaults for unspecified parameters was something like this,

```
function getSum(a,b) {
    a = (a !== undefined) ? a : 1;
    b = (b !== undefined) ? b : 41;

    console.log( a + b );
}

getSum();               // 42
getSum(1, 2);           // 3
getSum(10);             // 51
getSum(null, 6);        // 6
```

ES6 tries to streamline this process by giving us the ability to set a default value to the parameter in the function declaration statement itself.

```
var getSum2 = function(a = 1, b = 41) {
        console.log(a + b);
}

getSum2();              // 42
getSum2(1, 2);          // 3
getSum2(10);            // 51
getSum2(null, 6);       // 6
```

When we call the function, if we do not specify any argument, the default value of the parameter gets used. The syntax to specify a default value is the parameter followed by an equal sign "=" and an expression after that.

```
var getAnswer = function(number = 42, item = "universe") {
        console.log(number + " is the answer to " + item);
}
```

```
getAnswer(undefined, "life"); // 42 is the answer to life
```

Here, we are passing undefined as the first parameter, and ES6 will use the default value 42 instead.

Function default values can be more than just simple values like 42; they can be any valid expression, even a function call. You can use complex expressions as default values for parameters. Default value expressions are evaluated lazily, meaning they're run only if a parameter's argument is not present or is undefined.

```
var getName = function(firstName = "John", lastName = "Doe") {
        console.log(firstName + " " + lastName);
}
```

```
getName("Jane"); // Jane Doe
```

You can also access the other variables in the expression used as the default value.

```
var defaultName = "John";
```

```
var getName = function(firstName = defaultName, lastName = "Doe") {
        console.log(firstName + " " + lastName);
}
```

```
getName(); // John Doe
```

You can also access a function when specifying a default for an argument.

```
var getFirstName = () => "John";
```

```
var getName = function(firstName = getFirstName(), lastName = "Doe") {
        console.log(firstName + " " + lastName);

}
```

```
getName(); // John Doe
```

In the above few examples, if we try to check the number of arguments:

```
var getName = function(firstName, lastName = "Doe") {
    console.log(arguments.length);
}

getName("John"); // 1
```

Even though the second argument gets a default value, **arguments.length** only returns the number of arguments passed to it.

Let's take a look at a little more complicated example:

```
var getPrice = function(quantity = price, price = 5) {
    console.log(quantity + ", " + price);
}

getPrice(); // ReferenceError: price is not defined
```

Think of the function declaration and arguments like a scope. The parameters of a function declaration are in their own scope between the parentheses (...). Do not confuse this with the function body scope. JavaScript has not yet reached the price declaration when evaluating quantity and hence it does not know the value of price. The reference to an identifier in a default value expression first matches the formal parameters' scope before looking to an outer scope.

Like we discussed in the section on let declarations ES6 has a TDZ that does not allow the variable to be accessed before it is initialized. Therefore, in the above example a TDZ reference error occurs when you try to use a parameter before it is declared.

Another awesome feature of the default parameters in ES6 is the fact that they work even when creating a dynamic function:

```
var getNumber = new Function("number = 42", "return number;");
console.log(getNumber()); // 42
```

Rest and Spread Operators

JavaScript has always had the feature of allowing functions to be passes fewer or more parameters than formally specified in the function declaration without any problems. Default Parameters, as discussed earlier, help you accept fewer values as parameters and still have the other parameters assigned a value.

Many modern programming languages provide the ability for the function to accept a variable number of parameters. ES6 introduces this much needed feature to JavaScript with Rest Parameters. You now have the ability to pass a function a dynamic number of parameters very easily. If you wanted to do this in ES5 you would have to put all the values in a data container data type like an array. The Rest Parameters simplify this entire process.

■ **Note** Do not confuse this term to the web services concept of REST. This has nothing to do with REST in web services. Rest here refers to gathering up parameters and putting them all into a single array. Spread refers to spreading out the elements of an array (or even a string).

Let's look at an example,

```
var showCollections = function (id, ...collection) {
        console.log(collection instanceof Array);
};

showCollections(42, "movies", "music");  // true
```

The ... symbol is the rest symbol. It precedes a named parameter. This named parameter will become an Array that will just gather up all the remaining parameters passed to the function. Hence here, Collections is set to an array. To make this more clear if we execute the above program this way,

```
var showCollections = function (id, ...collection) {
        console.log(collection);
};

showCollections(42, "movies", "music"); // ["movies", "music"]
```

The Rest parameter gathers up all the remaining parameters after the id parameter and makes it into an array called collection. Excluding the first defined parameter 'id', everything will be placed in the Array.

If we call the same function by passing it just one value which is the id, it logs out an empty array [].

Let's look the length property of the function. If we call showCollections.length, it will give us the number of parameters in the function.

```
var showCollections = function (id, ...collection) {};
console.log(showCollections.length); // 1
```

The length property ignores the *Rest parameter*. In this case, it is 1. The length property of the function only counts the number of named parameters excluding the rest parameter. Now let's look at the case where we check the arguments.length inside the function:

```
var showCollections = function (id, ...collection) {
        console.log(arguments.length);
};

showCollections(123, "movies", "music"); // 3
```

We already had an arguments object, which we can use to check all the parameters passed to a function without having to define each parameter specifically. Remember we can have both named and unnamed parameters in a function. In this case, even though we have two parameters in the function definition, arguments object is going to refer back to the original function call and three is the number of arguments passed to the function.

In the ES4 specification, *Rest parameters* were meant to replace arguments and arguments object was completely done away with, but ES4 never came into being and in ES6, this concept was reintroduced, but this time the 'arguments' has not been removed from the language.

We can use the Rest operator in a function constructor. Check the following where we are creating a new function that has a rest parameter and returns the very first argument that is passed into it.

```
var getFirst = new Function("...args", "return args[0]");
console.log(getFirst(1, 2));    // 1
```

The Spread Operator

The spread operator, which is also denoted by ... before an array, does essentially the reverse operation of a rest operator. It spreads out an array and passes the values into the specified function. Consider the following example:

```
let values = [200, 300, 400];
let newSet = [100, ...values, 500]

console.log(newSet);  // [100, 200, 300, 400, 500]
```

The spread operator is very closely related to the rest parameters. In this particular format as a spread operator, ... is used like a concatenation or insertion mechanism where the values array is inserted in between existing values to assign the newly formed array to newSet.

In case of the rest parameters, you can combine multiple arguments into a single array, while in case of the spread operator you can specify a single array that can be split into separate arguments that can be passed into a function or method. Let us look at another example using the Math.max() method and the spread operator:

```
let numbers = [-25, 100, 42, -1000];
console.log(Math.max(...numbers, 900));        // 900
```

In the above case, Math.max is passed five arguments, the first four being -25, 100, 42, and -1000 and another fifth argument we added 900. The result is the maximum among them which is 900. Therefore, the spread operator spreads out the values in an array as arguments in a function call.

The spread operator helps in handling arguments to be passed to a function as arrays much easier. Just like the rest operator, you can use the spread operator in a function constructor as well.

If we try to spread out an empty array, which might be missing two values like [, ,] the last comma is considered a trailing comma that is ignored. The parameters spread out would also be undefined. Consider the following example:

```
function printInput(...input) {
        console.log(input);
}

let input = [,,];

printInput(...input); // [undefined, undefined]
```

Object Literal Extensions

ES6 introduces some new extensions for Object Literals.

To declare object literals, currently using variables we have to use the following coding pattern:

```
var price = 4.20, quantity = 20;
var invoiceData = {
        price: price,
quantity: quantity
};

console.log(invoiceData);
```

Declaring price and quantity twice is kind of redundant, but now ES6 offers a shorthand making writing this simpler. Check the following example:

```
const price = 4.20, quantity = 20;
const invoiceData = {
        price,
quantity
};

console.log(invoiceData);
```

We can just list the field once and the object literal in ES6 is smart enough to interpret that we want a field called price and want the context data set to the value of the variable called price. This shorthand notation reduces code and also makes it easier to read.

ES6 also gives us a short notation to write functions in an object literal. Check the following code snippet, for example:

```
const price = 4.20, quantity = 20;
const invoiceData = {
        price,
        quantity,
```

```
        calculateTotal() {
                return this.price * this.quantity;
        }
};
console.log(invoiceData.calculateTotal());
```

In the above shorthand notation, you no longer need the keyword function. When we use the function shorthand within an object literal, this refers to the context of the code just like an arrow function. It does not refer to the object that contains the function. It behaves exactly like an arrow function.

Note that you can use dynamic field names in an object literal:

```
const field = 'dynamicRandom';
const price = 5.99;
const quantity = 2;
const invoiceData = {
        [field]: price,
        quantity,
        calculateTotal() {
                return this.price * this.quantity;
        }
};

console.log(invoiceData);
// { dynamicRandom: 5.99,
//   quantity: 2,
//   caculateTotal: [Function: calculateTotal] }
```

The field in the object gets assigned the name dynamicField. You can actually use an entire expression and make naming properties even more dynamic:

```
const field = 'dynamicRandom';
const price = 5.99, quantity = 2;
const invoiceData = {
        [field + "-01"]: price,
        quantity,
        calculateTotal() {
                return this.price * this.quantity;
        }
};

console.log(invoiceData);
// { dynamicRandom-01: 5.99,
//   quantity: 2,
//   caculateTotal: [Function: calculateTotal] }
```

You can actually create a dynamic field name in a method as well. They work with setters and getters as well.

Template Literals and Delimiters

Strings in JavaScript have been historically limited, lacking the capabilities one might expect coming from other programming languages. ES6 introduces Template Literals, which provide you a way to define strings with additional functionalities like:

- String interpolation
- Embedded expressions
- Multiline strings without hacks
- String formatting

Template Literals use backticks (` `) rather than the single or double quotes. Template literals, in the end, always produce strings. A template literal can be written as follows:

```
let user = `Kevin`;
```

Template literals allow **string substitutions** that provide us a way to substitute any valid JavaScript expression inside a string. Template Literals can contain placeholders for string substitution using the ${ } syntax. Consider the following example:

```
console.log(`Hi ${user}!`); // Hi Kevin!
```

In the above example, the template literal is delimited by backticks (`) and the interpolated expressions inside the literal are delimited by ${ and }.

We can also substitute a lot more than variable names. Template Literals allow us to use **expression interpolation** to embed readable inline math, for example:

```
let a = 10;
let b = 20;

console.log(`Sum of ${a} and ${b} is ${a+b}`);
```

Template literals also allow you to add multiline strings easily (without the use of \n):

```
console.log(`I am line-one
I am line-two`);

// I am line-one
// I am line-two
```

Tagged Template Literals

A more advanced form of template literals are tagged template literals. Tagged Templates transform a Template String by placing a function name before the template string. For example:

```
output`Hi, my name is ${name} and I love ${language}`;
```

This expression can be transformed into a function call that takes two kinds of parameters:

1.   Array of literal strings, that is ["Hi, my name is", "and I love", " "]

2.   Substitutions, that is, name, language.

The total number of Literal Strings are always one greater than the number of Substitutions. You can consider each substitution wrapped around by two literals on each side. That's why there is an empty string as the last element in the array of literal strings above.

Therefore, the above tagged template can be written as:

```
output(["Hi, my name is ", " and I love ", ""], name, language)
```

The tag functions are typically defined using rest arguments to allow easier parameter handling. The above function can be defined as:

```
function output(literals, ...substitutions) {
        let result = "";

        // concatenate literal strings and substitutions
        for (let i=0; i<substitutions.length; i++) {
                result += literals[i] + substitutions[i];
        }

        // concatenate the last element in the literals array
        // there is always one element more than the substitutions array
        result += literals[literals.length - 1];

        return result;
}
const  name = 'John',
        language = 'JavaScript';

let text = output`Hi, my name is ${name} and I love ${language}`

console.log(text); // Hi, my name is John and I love JavaScript
```

Since these functions receive the parts of a Template String as arguments, you can then decide how to use the strings and substitutions to determine the final output of your string. For instance, you can use the output function to convert all the characters into uppercase, converge the input into a hash-string, or anything you may want.

Iterating with for...of

Over the last two decades in JavaScript, we have been iterating using the for, for-in, and forEach (in case of arrays). ES6 introduces another structure, the for...of loop, which allows iterating over iterable objects such as array, map, set, string, etc.

We will be looking at iterators and iterables more closely later in this book. Consider a simple for-loop for iterating over an array:

```
let names = ['matt', 'smith', 'jack'];

for (let i = 0; i<names.length; i++) {
    console.log(names[i]);
}
// matt
// smith
// jack
```

There's absolutely nothing wrong with this format, but with the new syntax, we don't have to initialize and keep track of the loop counter variable (i). We can achieve the same iteration logic with lesser and cleaner syntax. Check the following code snippet written using the for-of syntax:

```
let names = ['matt', 'smith', 'jack'];

for (let name of names) {
    console.log(name);
}
// matt
// smith
// jack
```

Note that the value you loop over using for...of must be an iterable. An iterable is simply an object that is able to produce an iterator, which the loop then uses. The for...of loop doesn't just work for arrays, but also other iterables like the DOM NodeList object, the arguments object, and String objects. Just like with arrays, the for-of loop makes it easier to iterate over these non-Array sequences. Consider the following code snippet, for example:

```
for (let char of 'Bye') {
    console.log(char);
}

// B
// y
// e
```

■ **Note**   It is important to not confuse for...of with the older for...in loop syntax, which is used to iterate over the enumerable properties (or keys) of an object.

The applications and advantages of the for...of loop structure will make much more sense when we discuss the iterators and iterables in detail later in this book. This section was merely meant to introduce the new for...of loop syntax and its usage with data structures like arrays and strings.

Summary

If you have been a JavaScript programmer, you might be aware of a few quirks in the way we write JavaScript even though it has a fairly reasonable and straightforward syntax similar to other languages. ES6 tries to address many of these issues by bringing in a lot of new syntax and changes to existing patterns in JavaScript. There are plenty of new concepts for you to become familiar with. Many of the new patterns introduced aim at addressing existing challenges in previous versions of the language and easing the process of programming in JavaScript. They help in writing cleaner code, debugging faster, implementing logic in fewer lines, and avoiding confusion.

New keywords like `let` and `const` for variable declarations introduce block scoping to JavaScript, bringing in functionality common to other programming languages, making it easier to write more robust code and aid in the process of debugging. Features like Arrow functions, while helping in writing shorter and nicer-looking functions, also bring in specific behaviors that you can use for particular situations, like making the use of the `this` keyword more simple.

Through this chapter, we also introduced to you new concepts like default values for function parameters and the Rest and Spread operators. The pattern of gathering the "rest" of the parameters of a function into an array is now merely using three dots. We also discussed how template literals grant us more power for templating and string manipulations. Finally, we looked at the new `for...of` loop structure for iterating over the iterables without having to use an additional counter variable.

We have only introduced a few new important syntax features in this chapter, but over the course of the next few chapters, we will be looking at many more new features like Destructuring, Classes and Modules, Iterators and Generators, Meta Programming, etc. So stay tuned.

CHAPTER 3

Destructuring

Object literals and arrays are probably some of the most widely used notations in JavaScript. The popularity of these JavaScript notations is further extended to even outside the language with their presence in the JSON data format. Objects and arrays are commonly used to group data in JavaScript and there exists various patterns to systematically fetch data from these defined structures when we need them. ES6 further extends this process by making it easier and simpler through a process called *destructuring*.

Destructuring of Objects and Arrays

Destructuring is basically a convenient way of breaking the data structure into smaller pieces to access its data more easily and extract multiple values from Objects or Arrays. To understand destructuring better, simply think of it as a structured assignment from an object or array. Consider the following example,

```
var letters = ['a', 'b', 'c'],
    x = letters[0],
    y = letters[1],
    z = letters[2];

console.log( x, y, z );          // a b c
```

In the above example, we assigned values to an array called letters and then the x, y, and z variables using indices on the letters variable. Let us look at another such example using objects:

```
var numbers = {a: 1, b: 2, c: 3},
    a = numbers.a,
    b = numbers.b,
    c = numbers.c;

console.log( a, b, c );          // 1 2 3
```

In this example, we use the numbers.a value to assign the value of the variable a and similarly numbers.b & numbers.c for b and c variables. ES6 makes this pattern of structured assignment simpler through a new and dedicated syntax called *destructuring*.

© Deepak Grover and Hanu Kunduru 2017

D. Grover and H. P. Kunduru, *ES6 for Humans*, DOI 10.1007/978-1-4842-2623-0_3

This syntax eliminates the need for the temporary, intermediate variables – letters and numbers. Consider the following examples:

```
var [ x, y, z ] = ['a', 'b', 'c'];
var { a: a, b: b, c: c } = {a: 1, b: 2, c: 3};

console.log( x, y, z );          // a b c
console.log( a, b, c );          // 1 2 3
```

■ **Note**   We are commonly used to seeing an object and array syntax like {a: a, b:b, c:c } and [x, y, z] on the right side of an assignment statement. Destructuring flips this pattern and puts them on the left side with a variable declaration keyword, and lets you decompose the right side into individual values to be assigned to the variables on the left side.

As seen in the previous two examples, prior to ES6, fetching information from objects and arrays and putting them into local variables needed a lot more code. Imagine you needed to extract values from a very large object or array and store them in variables of the same name. You would have to write a lot of code assigning values to them one by one, but using destructuring, this process gets reduced to a single assignment statement.

Breaking the data structure into smaller parts using destructuring makes fetching the data you need much easier. Furthermore, destructuring in ES6 uses the object and array literal notation syntax, which traditional users of JavaScript are already familiar with.

Object Destructuring Syntax

Let us take a look at the object destructuring syntax a little more closely. The Object Destructuring syntax as we have seen is,

```
var { a: a, b: b, c: c } = {a: 1, b: 2, c: 3};
```

In this example, you can notice that we used the same name for the variables being assigned and the properties of the returned object. They do not have to be the same, though, you can use any name for the local variables being assigned. But in case they are the same, the syntax can be further shortened by leaving out the "a: " part of the notation. This declaration statement can simply be written as,

```
var { a, b, c } = {a: 1, b: 2, c: 3};

console.log( a, b, c );             // 1 2 3
```

It makes a lot of sense for us to use the smaller syntax instead of the long form, unless you want to assign a property to a different variable name, but there is an important nuance you need to be careful about when using the long form. Consider the following example,

```
var { a: foo, b: bar, c: baz } = {a: 1, b: 2, c: 3};

console.log( foo, bar, baz );        // 1 2 3
console.log( a, b, c );              // ReferenceError
```

Observe this example closely. The pattern may seem very straightforward where the left side gets the values from the right side inside the object notation { a: foo, b: bar, c: baz }. But it is actually the other way around. It is not the "*target: source*" pattern we are commonly used to, but more accurately it is the inverse, that is, the "*source: target*" pattern. Why this confusion though? This pattern will make more sense if you look at it in a different way. Consider the following assignment:

```
var foo = 42, bar = 100;

var obj = { a: foo, b: bar };
var { a: FOO, b: BAR } = obj;

console.log( FOO, BAR );             // 42 100
```

In this example, a and b refer to the properties of the object and in the object destructuring assignment statement, a and b also represent the object properties. Remember how in a previous example where we shortened the code, we said we could leave out the a: part. It is precisely for this reason. In this example, if you get rid of the a: and b: sections of the syntax, you will be left with FOO and BAR. This syntax can sometimes be confusing, but it can be simple to grasp it,\ if you think of it as corresponding property names and values being mapped to each other: in this case foo get assigned to FOO and bar to BAR using the a and b property names.

Using Object Destructuring, you can actually set the value of multiple variables using the same property value. Consider the following example:

```
var { x: foo, x: bar } = { x: 42 };

console.log( foo );  // 42
console.log( bar );  // 42
```

In this case both foo and bar get their value using the x property of the object.

You are free to use let, const, or var depending on the situation and requirement in a destructuring declaration statement. But be sure to always have an assignment in the statement, that is, a right-hand side is required for the statement.

```
var { x, y };          // syntax error!
let { x, y };          // syntax error!
const { x, y };        // syntax error!
```

All of the above declarations result in a syntax error because of a missing initializer in the destructuring declaration. While we know that const requires an initializer in all cases, when using destructuring var and let, they also require initializers.

Assignment Using Destructuring

So far in our discussion we have only seen cases where we use destructuring declarations statements. But destructuring can also be used in assignment statements. Consider the following example using getChars() and getNumbers() functions from the previous examples,

```
var a, b, c, x, y, z;

[x, y ,z] = getChars();
( { a, b, c } = getNumbers() );

console.log( x, y, z );           // a b c
console.log( a, b, c );           // 1 2 3
```

In this example the x, y, z, a, b, and c are all assigned using destructuring after they are declared.

■ **Note**   You must always use parentheses around an object destructuring assignment statement. This is because an opening curly brace is used to denote the start of a block statement. The parentheses around it denote that the curly brace should be interpreted as an expression used in an assignment statement using destructuring.

You can also change the values of variables after they are assigned using destructuring. Consider the following example,

```
let item = {
        name: "Apples",
        quantity: 5
    },
    name = "Oranges",
    quantity = 3;

// assigning different values using destructuring
({ name, quantity } = item);

console.log(name);        // "Apples"
console.log(quantity);    // 5
```

In this example, name, quantity, and item are initialized with values in a single declaration statement. Then name and quantity are assigned new values by fetching values from item using destructuring.

Default Values

When using destructuring to assign a value to a variable using an object that does not have the corresponding property name, its value is set to undefined. For example:

```
var item = {
        name: "Apples",
        quantity: 5
};
var { name, quantity, value } = item;
console.log(name);          // "Apples"
console.log(quantity);      // 5
console.log(value);         // undefined
```

In this example, an extra variable value that does not have a corresponding property inside item is declared in the destructuring statement. It gets set to undefined while name and quantity get their respective values from item.

Additionally, instead of giving the extra variables a value of undefined, you can also choose to define a default value in case of the absence of the specified property. To do so, just use an equals sign (=) after the property name and specify a default value, like this:

```
var item = {
        name: "Apples",
        quantity: 5
};

var { name = "Oranges", quantity = 3, value = 25 } = item;

console.log(name);          // "Apples"
console.log(quantity);      // 5
console.log(value);         // 25
```

In this example, the variables quantity and value are given 3 and 25 as their default values respectively. Since there is no item.value property, the variable value uses its default value 25. This works similarly to the default parameter values for functions that we saw in the previous chapter.

■ **Note**   The default value (or undefined if not specified) will only be assigned to the variable in case of a missing property in the item.

You can also use default values in the long form of a destructuring assignment statement. But at this point the code can start getting dirty and a little confusing. Consider the following example:

```
var { a, b, c: c = 3, d: FOO = 42 } = {a: 1, b: 2};
console.log( a, b, c, FOO );     // 1 2 3 42
```

In this case, the variables a and b are declared and set to their corresponding property values from the object literal on the right-hand side, but since the property c does not exist in this object, its value is set to the default value of 3. The declared variable FOO is also set to its default value 42 since the corresponding property d is not present in the object. Here is where you need to remember the "*target:source*" syntax we discussed above, which can sometimes lead to confusion. So it might be best to avoid this mixed coding style unless absolutely necessary.

Another suggestion we have is to avoid using an object or array as the default value inside a destructuring statement. This also can lead to confusion for anyone reading your code, including yourself. Take a look at the following example:

```
var a = 1, b = 2, c = 3;
var obj = { a: { b: 42 }, c: { b: c } };

( { b: a = { b: b } } = obj );
( { c: b = { b: c } } = obj );
( { a: c = { b: a } } = obj );

console.log( a.b, b.b, c.b );
```

Try guessing what would be the output of the `console.log` statement. Full credit to you if you guessed "2 3 42." But you get the idea why this can be confusing.

Nested Destructuring

The destructuring syntax, very much like the Object Literal syntax, can be used to navigate inside nested objects to retrieve information. If the values you're destructuring have nested objects or arrays, you can destructure those nested values as well. Here's an example:

```
let items = {
    count : 2,
    name: "fruits",
    apple: {
        quantity: 5,
        value: 25
    },
    orange: {
        quantity: 3,
        value: 5
    }
};

let { apple: { quantity }} = items;

console.log(quantity);        // 5
```

Curly braces here are used to denote that we have to first go down one level to the apple property inside the items object and then fetch the property quantity. From our previous discussion, we know that the identifier before the ' : ' denotes the location we need to go to and the right side assigns a value. If a curly brace is present after the colon, it denotes that the destination is nested in the next depth level of the object and so on.

Since empty curly braces can be legal in object destructuring, you have to be very careful while using nested destructuring. Consider the following example:

```
let { apple: {} } = items;
console.log(apple);        // ReferenceError: apple is not defined
```

This destructuring statement has no bindings and because of the curly braces on the right, apple is not a variable binding to create but rather is used as a location to inspect inside the items object. In this case, if you wanted to create binding for the variable apple, it would make sense to use = to define a default value rather than : that defines a location, for example:

```
let { apple = {} } = items;
console.log(apple);        // {quantity: 5, value: 25}
```

Let us take another example using nested array destructuring. You can insert another array pattern into the overall pattern and the destructuring will descend into a nested array:

```
let fruits = [ "apple", [ "blueberry", "raspberry" ], "orange" ];

let [ fruit1, [ fruit2 ], fruit4 ] = fruits;

console.log(fruit1);      // "apple"
console.log(fruit2);      // "blueberry"
console.log(fruit4);      // "orange"
```

In this example, the variable fruit2 will be assigned the value "blueberry" obtained from inside the second array denoting berries present within the fruits array. The extra square brackets in the destructuring statement around fruit2 are required to unpack the fruits array and the berries array present inside it. Similar to objects we have seen above, you can have any depth of nested arrays and will need to have corresponding notations in the destructuring statements to fetch values from within them.

We can build complex expressions for the destructuring of objects and arrays to fetch the right values and assign them to different variables, no matter how deep the object or array is nested or from a mixture of objects and arrays using just one statement with the power of destructuring. Consider the following example:

```
let student = {
    name: "Tony",
    courses: {
        english: {
            id: 1,
            score: 7
        },
```

43

```
        math: {
            id: 2,
            score: 9
        }
    },
    scoreRange: [0, 10]
};

let {
    courses: { english },
    scoreRange: [ minScore ]
} = student;

console.log(english.id);        // 1
console.log(english.score);     // 7
console.log(minScore);          // 0
```

This code extracts student.courses.english and student.scoreRange[0] into english and minScore, respectively. In this example both courses and scoreRange are variables in the destructured pattern that get their values from the corresponding properties within the student object. This sort of approach is extremely useful when you want to fetch some specific data or values from complex JSON structures without having to traverse through the whole tree.

Destructuring Using the rest Syntax

Using the rest operators along with the destructuring pattern can be a very powerful concise syntax to variable assignments in ES6. We have already explored the rest pattern in the previous chapter. Now let us take a look at it in conjunction with the destructing pattern. Consider the following example:

```
var num1, num2, rest;
var x, y, z;

[num1, num2, ...rest] = [1, 2, 3, 4, 5];
[x, y, z] = [1, 2, 3, 4, 5];

console.log(num1);      // 1
console.log(num2);      // 2
console.log(rest);      // [3, 4, 5]
console.log(x, y, z)    // 1 2 3
```

In the above example, using destructuring we assign values to the variables num1, num2, and rest (using the rest operator for only rest). We do the exact same for another set of variables x, y, and z. But if you notice the output when we assign values using an array containing five numbers, the first two values get assigned to num1 and num2, but the remaining ones get gathered into an array and get assigned to the variable rest because we used a rest operator along with it. Compare this to the second destructuring statement where only the value 3 is assigned to z.

An important point note here is the fact that a SyntaxError will be thrown if a trailing comma is used on the left-hand side with a rest element. Look the following example:

```
var [a, b,] = [1, 2, 3];
console.log(a, b)                    // 1 2
var [num1, ...num2,] = [1, 2, 3];
// SyntaxError: rest element may not have a trailing comma
```

Therefore, keep in mind that even though a trailing comma in a simple destructuring statement does not make any difference, you should not use it after the rest element in the destructuring statement.

Destructured Parameters

Apart from giving us a simpler declaration and assignment syntax, the destructuring syntax also can be used while passing function parameters. All the previously discussed variations of destructuring are available to us with parameter destructuring as well. Destructuring also mixes well with other ES6 function parameter capabilities, like default parameter values and rest parameters.

Let us take a look at a simple example using destructured array parameters:

```
function sum( [ num1, num2 = 0 ] ) {
    console.log( num1 + num2 );
}

sum( [ 1, 2 ] );           // 3
sum( [ 1 ] );              // 1
sum( [ ] );                // NaN
```

In the above example, there are multiple things to note: the sum() function when passed in an array of two values 1 and 2 prints their sum 3, but when passed only one value 1, it outputs 1 due to the fact that num2 has a default value of 0 assigned. When no value is passed to the destructured array, it prints NaN (Not a Number) because even though num2 defaults to 0, num1 is set to undefined.

When you need to provide a function with a large set of parameters, a common pattern is to create an object with properties specifying the parameters and passing the object into the function. But the problem with this pattern is the fact that it is incredibly hard to guess what input the function requires just by looking at the function definition. You will have to go over the body of the function to be able to understand the different inputs required by the function. Consider the following example where the function takes in an options object:

```
function createObj(name, value, options) {
    let obj = {};
    obj.x = options.a;
    obj.y = options.b;
```

```
    obj.z = options.c;
    obj[name] = value;
    return obj;
}

let options = {a: 1, b: 2, c: 3};
let testObj = createObj('test', 4, options);
console.log(testObj)// {x:1, y:2, z:3, test:4}
```

Here, the options object is one of the parameters required by the function createObj, but destructuring can help to better read and fetch the required properties of options needed inside the function. We can rewrite the function definition using destructured parameters as follows:

```
function createObj(name, value, {x:a, y:b, z:c}) {
    // code to return object
}
```

This function behaves exactly like the previous example, but since the third argument uses destructuring to fetch the corresponding values from the options object, it is easy to understand what inputs are required by the function just by looking at the function definition. Also the values can be assigned within the function call statement itself. Therefore, you can use default values, mixed object, and array patterns and also variable names that are different from the properties you read from.

■ **Note** Destructured parameters act like regular parameters in the sense that they are set to undefined if not passed.

The ability to use Object Destructured parameters brings to us an added bonus. They provide us with the ability to have optional parameters in any position of the list of parameters. Consider the following example,

```
function printNums( { num1, num2 } ) {
    console.log( num1, num2 );
}

printNums( { num2: 1, num1: 2 } );          // 2 1
printNums( { num2: 42 } );                   // undefined 42
```

In this example, the printNums() function prints two numbers passed into a destructured object as parameter having properties num1 and num2. Notice in the first function call how you can switch the order of the parameters by specifying num2 first and then num1. Similarly, by specifying only num2, you can actually set the value of the first intended parameter num1 as undefined.

At this juncture, it is important to point out the difference in behavior between a destructuring default value and a function parameter default value. Consider this example:

```
function foo({ num1 = 42 } = {}, { num2 } = { num2: 42 }) {
    console.log( num1, num2 );
}
foo();                          // 42 42
foo( {}, {} );                  // 42 undefined
```

In this example, if you do not pay attention to the output, it might seem like we have declared a default value of 42 for both num1 and num2 in two different ways. The first function call also indicates the same. But the second function call, where two empty objects are passed into the function, tells a different story.

If you observe closely, there is a subtle difference in the two ways of declaring the values of the parameters. In the above example, the function foo takes two parameters:

- { num1 = 42 } = {}

- { num2 } = { num2: 42 }

When no argument is passed to the function, the first parameter defaults to an empty object {}, but since it uses object destructuring, the named parameter num1 defaults to 42, both in this case and also when the object passed in as an argument does not have num1 as a property.

In the case of the second argument, the default parameter value is an object { num2: 42 }. The parameter defaults to this object when there is no second argument provided to the function. Because of the destructured object on the left-hand side, when the parameter defaults to the object, num2 is set to 42. But in the case where an empty object {} is passed as a second argument, the default value is never used, and the { num2 } destructuring occurs against the passed in {} empty object value, resulting in num2 set to undefined.

Summary

As you move around data in JavaScript, you will start appreciating the need to extract specific pieces of information by breaking down objects and arrays to examine their components individually. Prior to ES6, developers needed to write quite a bit of code to destructure their data, but now they can enjoy the new syntax ES6 brings for destructuring, making the process a lot simpler in terms of the amount of code they have to write.

Furthermore, destructuring helps in making object parameters of a function more explicit. Using destructuring, you can have default values without having to check if the property is present in the object, and we can now make optional properties more explicit by providing a default value for a property. Explicitly visible things make code easier to maintain, as you don't have to guess or read the whole function to figure it out.

CHAPTER 4

■ ■ ■

Classes in ES6

If you are coming from object oriented programming languages like C++, Java, or Python, you must already be aware of how classes work. Prior to ES6, classes never existed in JavaScript, but from the early days, many patterns have existed to emulate classical class-oriented development. The concept of classes was teased in various different forms, primarily due to the fact that classes and classical inheritance could not be supported inside JavaScript in a clean straightforward way. This left a lot of traditional developers from other languages confused because classes and inheritance in JavaScript are not the primary method of creating similar or related objects.

The syntax and coding patterns tried to use class-oriented development in hidden ways inside the prototype system with things like new, instanceOf, and the constructor property. Many libraries like JSClass, Classify.js, etc., existed to make JavaScript feel like it supported traditional classes. Hence even though a lot of conventional JS developers did not think there was a need for Classes in its traditional sense, just the sheer number of libraries influenced TC39 to introduce "classes" in ES6. The goal was to make them look similar to real classes, which was done by introducing the class keyword and a related mechanism for declaring them.

Classes in ES6

The class pattern was widely debated and argued on through the design process of ES6 and a compromise was reached. It is important here to understand that ES6 classes do not work exactly the same way as in other object oriented languages. That said, TC39 is still in the process of adding more features post-ES6 to augment classes to bring them closer to the classical definition.

Conceptually, there is no Class in traditional JavaScript. A class in ES6 is simply a function under the hood. It is nothing more than syntactical sugar over Objects and Prototypes, offering a convenient declarative form for class patterns that encourage interoperability. This new class keyword in ES6 supports prototype-based inheritance, constructors, super calls, instance, and static methods.

Let's look at how you'd write the most basic form of class declaration in ES6, which is very similar to how classes are defined in other languages. Consider the following example:

```
class Car {
    constructor(brand) {
        this.brand = brand;
```

© Deepak Grover and Hanu Kunduru 2017

D. Grover and H. P. Kunduru, *ES6 for Humans*, DOI 10.1007/978-1-4842-2623-0_4

```
    }
}
```

```
const myTesla = new Car("Tesla");
```

```
console.log(myTesla.hasOwnProperty("brand"));  // true
```

```
console.log(typeof Car);                        // function
```

In this example, brand is the property assigned on the myTesla object. This object can also be represented in an object literal form as follows:

```
const myTesla = {
    brand: "Tesla"
};
```

The above example is a simple representation of how you can create a class with an optional constructor method that will be called when an object of this class is instantiated. Classes in ES6 don't add any functionality to what we already have in the language; they are just a simpler syntax for building the objects. Any arguments passed into new Car() will be received as parameters to the constructor method of Car, and you can use those parameters to initialize instances of the same class. Therefore, the constructor() method is where you initialize your object's properties and these properties are enumerable. Also, since the constructor() method is optional, you can declare an empty class like the one in the following example:

```
class EmptyClass {

}
```

If you don't define a constructor() method inside a class, the JavaScript engine will insert an empty one for you:

```
class EmptyClass {

    /* JavaScript inserts an empty constructor:
     constructor () { }
    */

}
```

Now that we know how and where to initialize properties in a class, let's look at how you can define methods. Class declarations allow you to define methods on a class without the use of a "function" keyword:

```
class Car {
        constructor(brand) {
                this.brand = brand;
```

```
    }

    start() {
            console.log(`Your ${this.brand} is ready to go!`);
    }
}

const myTesla = new Car("Tesla");

myTesla.start();
// Your Tesla is ready to go!
```

In the above example, we defined a start() method inside the class definition, which accesses the brand property of the class using this keyword. This method gets automatically attached to the class's prototype and hence is non-enumerable. We will discuss this and class methods in greater detail later in this chapter, but first, let's take a look at the different ways in which we can define classes in ES6.

Defining Classes in ES6

Just like in the case of functions, there are two ways in which you can define classes in ES6. Let us look at each of them.

Class Declarations

As seen in the previous example, class declarations are pretty simple. You declare a class using the "class" keyword followed by a class-name, which is generally by convention written in TitleCase. A good thing to note here is that the name of a class behaves as if it is a constant inside the class definition, which means you cannot overwrite a class using the class name inside itself:

```
class SimpleClass {
    constructor() {
        SimpleClass = "42";        // throws an error during execution
    }
}

SimpleClass = "42";                // works fine after the declaration
```

Unlike function declarations, class declarations are not hoisted. Similar to let and const, class declarations reside in the temporal dead zone (TDZ) until the execution reaches the point of class declaration. Therefore, you need to declare your class before accessing it, otherwise a ReferenceError will occur:

```
const b = new Bike(); // ReferenceError

class Bike {}
```

In the above example, since the class has not already been declared, it exists in the TDZ and so when you try to initialize a new instance using the new keyword, a reference error is thrown.

Class Expressions

Apart from Class declarations, the second way of defining new classes in ES6 is through Class Expressions. They are identical to function expressions, and just like function expressions they can also be anonymous. Consider the following example:

```
const Circle = class {
        constructor() {
                this.radius = 20;
        }
}
```

Notice, in the above example, how the identifier is missing after the class keyword; this makes it an anonymous class expression. Besides variable declarations, these class expressions can also be used to be pass arguments into functions. Consider the following code snippet that has a factory function to create cars:

```
function carFactory(car) {
        return new car();
}

const Toyota  = carFactory(class {
        start() {
                console.log("Your car is ready to roll");
        }
        stop() {
                console.log("Shutting down the engines");
        }
});

Toyota.start();
// Your car is ready to roll

Toyota.stop();
// Shutting down the engines
```

The factory function takes in the class definition as an argument and returns the object of the class passed in as the argument. In programming languages, if an entity can be passed as an argument, returned from a function, modified, and assigned to a variable, it is considered to be a first-class citizen of the language. One of the many reasons that functional programming is popular with JavaScript is because of functions being the first-class citizen of the language, allowing us to use functions to the fullest extent and easily creating higher order functions. In ES6, similar to functions, classes are also the first-class citizens of the language, allowing a class to be passed as an argument to functions, as seen in the above example, and assigned to a variable using class expressions.

Class Methods and Accessor Properties

Prior to ES6 you needed the Object.defineProperty() to make a method non-enumerable, but in ES6 all methods of a class are non-enumerable. These methods are attached to the prototype, which enables the method to be shared by all instances of the class, providing an efficient way to conserve memory.

The syntax for defining methods of a class in ES6 is similar to the object literal method shorthand (i.e., functions without the function keyword):

```
class AeroPlane {
        constructor(model, capacity) {
                this.model = model;
                this.capacity = capacity;
        }
        getData() {
                console.log(`You're flying a ${this.model} aeroplane`);
                console.log(`This plane can fly with ${this.capacity}
                passengers`);
        }
}

const jet = new AeroPlane("Jet", 60);

jet.getData();
// You're flying a Jet aeroplane
// This plane can fly with 60 passengers

console.log(jet.hasOwnProperty("getData"));                    // false
console.log(jet.__proto__.hasOwnProperty("getData"));          // true
```

The above example shows a class AeroPlane where we initialize the instance properties named model and capacity upon construction of each instance. The getData() method declaration tells the instances of our AeroPlane class that they will have a getData() method, which will return the results of this method, whenever that method is called. This getData() method gets automatically added to the prototype. The ES5 way to re-create the above example would be:

```
function AeroPlane(model, capacity) {
        this.model = model;
        this.capacity = capacity;
}

AeroPlane.prototype.getData = function() {
        console.log("You're flying a " + this.model + " aeroplane");
        console.log("This plane can fly with " + this.capacity + "
        passengers");
}
```

```
var jet = new AeroPlane("Jet", 60);

jet.getData();

// You're flying a Jet aeroplane
// This plane can fly with 60 passengers
```

ES6 classes also allow you to create accessor properties on the prototype. We can use get and set keywords before the identifiers to create getter and setter properties respectively. These property descriptors are non-enumerable and can be accessed using Object.getOwnPropertyDescriptor() on the class's prototype, since these properties reside on the prototype object. Consider the following code snippet, for example:

```
class AeroPlane {
    constructor(model, capacity) {
        this._model = model;
        this._capacity = capacity;
    }

    get model() {
        return this._model;
    }

    get capacity() {
        return this._capacity;
    }

    set model(model) {
        this._model = model;
    }

    set capacity(capacity) {
        this._capacity = capacity;
    }
}

const jet = new AeroPlane("Jet", 100);

console.log(jet.capacity);
// 100

console.log(Object.getOwnPropertyDescriptor(AeroPlane.prototype, "model"));

/*
{
    get: [Function: get model],
    set: [Function: set model],
    enumerable: false,
```

```
    configurable: true
}
*/
```

In the above example, you must note that we have added an _ (underscore) before property names inside the class definition. Let's take a look at why we did that, using the following code snippet:

```
class StudyGroup {
        constructor(name) {
                this.name = name;
        }

        set name(newName) {
        this.name = newName;
        }
}

const jsGroup = new StudyGroup("js");

// RangeError: Maximum call stack size exceeded
```

If you try to run the above code snippet, you would see a RangeError stating Maximum call stack size exceeded, which is because of your setter property recursively setting itself, going into an infinite function call. Therefore, you must never have your setter method name the same as that of your property because accessing the property setter by its own name inside the setter creates an infinite recursive function call.

At this point, if you're wondering why use setters and getters in the first place, here are some reasons why you should consider using them:

- Setters and getters allow us to encapsulate the behavior associated with getting or setting of the object's property, which makes the code more extendible as you can easily add more functionalities like validation of the input or some transformations of the input data based on your needs. Also, it can be helpful to inherit these validation or transformation functionalities to child classes and have them in place or modify as per the application's needs.

- At times, it may seem like a good idea to have an alternate representation of the property exposed to the user via property accessors, hiding the internal representation of the property.

- Having property accessor methods allow us to set different access levels, for example, the getter can be public but the setter method could be protected for certain group of users.

You should also note that the setter must have exactly one formal parameter, which means you should create individual setters and getters for each property of the class instance.

Computed Method Names

Similar to object literals, methods inside a class can have computed names. This also applies to getter and setter accessor properties of the class. As seen with object literals, the computed method names can be wrapped with [ ]; check the following code snippet for an example:

```
const methodName = "getColor";
const propName = "color";

class AeroPlane {
constructor(color) {
            this._color = color
      }

      [methodName]() {
            return this._color;
      }

      get [propName]() {
            return this[`_${propName}`];
      }

      set [propName](value) {
            return this[`_${propName}`] = value;
      }
}

const whiteJet = new AeroPlane("white");

console.log(whiteJet.color);
// white
```

In the above example, we are computing the method name and getter and setter accessor property names inside the class definition by wrapping them with [ ]. We are also using the string literals to evaluate the dynamic property name inside the getter and setter methods.

Class Properties and Privacy

So far, we have seen how we can add properties to a class's instance by defining the property inside the constructor method in the class definition. However, all the properties we have seen so far are public properties, which can be accessed easily outside the class definition without using the setter or getter methods. There has been a long-term discussion around private properties in the JavaScript community. Unfortunately, prior to ES6, private properties never existed in JavaScript so they had to be faked. And the most common convention was to prefix the property or method name with an underscore, which we saw in the previous example.

With ES6, there are a couple of ways for managing data privacy inside a class.

Using Constructor Environments

The idea of having methods and properties stored inside the constructor environment, capturing the variables in a closure, ensures that these methods or properties would not be added to the prototype and are only accessible to the constructor and to the functions it created.

```
class AeroPlane {
        constructor(capacity) {
                this.checkCapacity = function(value) {
                        if (capacity >= value) {
                                return true;
                        }
                        return false;
                }
        }
}
const jet = new AeroPlane(200);

console.log(jet.checkCapacity(100));    // true

console.log(jet.capacity);              // undefined
```

In the above example, the constructor environment stores the parameters and local variables, keeping class properties (here, capacity) private by making it inaccessible outside the constructor. This keeps the private data completely safe and inaccessible from the class's instance.

Using WeakMaps

Before we move forward to see how WeakMaps help in keeping the data private inside classes, let's take a quick look at what WeakMaps are. A WeakMap is a new data type introduced in ES6. They are simply a collection of keys and values with the main constraint of having an object as the keys. We will be learning more about them in detail later in this book. But for now, you should note that you can create a WeakMap using the following:

```
const myMap = new WeakMap();
```

and you can use set and get methods on the returned WeakMap to store and retrieve a value associated with it:

```
const myMap = new WeakMap();

const myObj = { name: "jack" };
```

```
myMap.set(myObj, "developer");

console.log(myMap.get(myObj));
// developer
```

As seen in the above code snippet, we are using an object as the key to store a value inside a WeakMap.

One of the other features of WeakMaps is that they do not prevent garbage collection in case there would be no other reference to the object. Therefore, using WeakMap to store properties of a class helps in keeping the data private, and it destroys those private properties whenever an instance associated with the class is destroyed.

```
const data = new WeakMap();

class AeroPlane {
    constructor(seats) {
        data.set(this, {
            capacity: seats
        });
    }

    get seats() {
        return data.get(this).capacity;
    }

    set seats(value) {
        data.get(this).capacity = value;
    }
}

const jet = new AeroPlane(200);
console.log(jet.capacity);              // undefined
console.log(jet.seats);                 // 200
```

In the above example, we are using a WeakMap to keep the data private and exposing setters and getters to interact with the private data of the class. But it comes at the cost of keeping your WeakMap hidden from the outside world. As long as it is hidden from outside access, your properties will remain safe and private.

Besides WeakMaps, ES6 also provides another new technique to keep the data private (or rather, prevent it from casual access) using Symbols, which we will learn later in this book.

Static Methods and Properties

With classes, you can also define properties and methods that are a part of a class and not particularly any instance of that class. These methods and properties are associated with the class, and not with the instances of the class, which is often useful in creating utility functions for an application. ES6 allows you to easily create static methods by using the static keyword before the method name:

```
class AeroPlane {
        constructor(capacity) {
                this.capacity = capacity;
        }

        static radio(message) {
                console.log(`Message from broadcast: ${message}`)
        }
}

AeroPlane.radio("Sky is clear");
// Message from broadcast: Sky is clear
```

As mentioned before, it is important to note that the static methods and properties are accessed directly from their class, and you cannot access a static method or property from the instance of the class. Therefore, static methods also cannot access the properties or methods defined on an instance of the class using this.

At the time of writing this book, ES6 does not support creating properties with static keywords. There is a proposal for adding them to the language specification, but until this proposal is accepted and the implementation gets released, you can either use static getters and setters or manually attach a static property to a class as follows:

```
class AeroPlane {
        constructor(capacity) {
                this.capacity = capacity;
        }
}

AeroPlane.color = "white";

console.log(AeroPlane.color);
// white

console.log(AeroPlane.capacity);
// undefined
```

In this example, notice how we are able to access the static property using the class-name, and it returns undefined on a non-static property.

Class Inheritance and the Super Keyword

ES6 introduces the extends keyword to allow creation of a class as a child of another class. Inheritance lets us incorporate another class's state and behavior into our own. Extending a class from its parent class prevents code duplication. Consider the following example:

```
class AeroPlane {
        constructor(capacity) {
```

```
                this.capacity = capacity;
        }

        showCapacity() {
                console.log(`Capacity of this plane: ${this.capacity}`);
        }
}

class FighterPlane {
        constructor(capacity) {
                this.capacity = capacity;
        }

        showCapacity() {
                console.log(`Capacity of this plane: ${this.capacity}`);
        }

        fire() {
                console.log("Loading weapons and firing");
        }
}
```

In the above example, the data property capacity and the method showCapacity are repeated between both of the classes. We can easily eliminate this duplication by having FighterPlane inherit from AeroPlane, allowing the state and behavior of AeroPlane to be incorporated into the FighterPlane. Consider the following example where class FighterPlane inherits from the parent class AeroPlane using the extends keyword:

```
class AeroPlane {
        constructor(capacity) {
                this.capacity = capacity;
        }

        showCapacity() {
                console.log(`Capacity of this plane: ${this.capacity}`);
        }
}

class FighterPlane extends AeroPlane {
        fire() {
                console.log("Loading weapons and firing");
        }
}

const phantom = new FighterPlane(2);

phantom.showCapacity();
// Capacity of this plane: 2
```

```
phantom.fire();
// Loading weapons and firing
```

If you wish to define a constructor method in derived classes as well, you would need to use super(), which allows the parent class's constructor to be called in the derived class. super() is responsible for initializing the context, therefore, you must call super() before accessing the context (this) inside the constructor method; otherwise it will result in an error.

If no constructor is defined, then super() is automatically called for with all the given arguments when a new instance of the class is created, as in the following example:

```
class FighterPlane extends AeroPlane {
        // no constructor

        fire() {
                console.log("Loading weapons and firing");
        }
}

// is equivalent to

class FighterPlane extends AeroPlane {
        constructor(...args) {
                super(...args);
        }

        fire() {
                console.log("Loading weapons and firing");
        }
}
```

Inheriting Static Properties

ES6 allows us to inherit static properties of a parent class into a child class. Consider the following example where a static method of AeroPlane is called on its derived class (FighterPlane):

```
class AeroPlane {
  static radio() {
       console.log("Radio works");
  }
}

class FighterPlane extends AeroPlane {}

FighterPlane.radio();
// Radio works
```

In this code, a new static `radio()` method is added to the AeroPlane class. Using inheritance, this method is available as `FighterPlane.radio()` and behaves in the same manner as the `AeroPlane.radio()` method.

Method Overriding

The methods of the parent class can easily be shadowed with the same name on the parent class, inside the derived class. For instance, check the following code snippet where `fly()` method from the parent class (AeroPlane) is being overridden inside the derived class (FighterPlane):

```
class AeroPlane {
      constructor(capacity) {
             this.capacity = capacity;
      }

      showCapacity() {
             console.log(`Capacity of this plane: ${this.capacity}`);
      }

      fly() {
             console.log("Engines on, and the plane will take off soon");
      }
}

class FighterPlane extends AeroPlane {
      fly() {
             console.log("Engines on, and the plane is gone");
      }

      fire() {
             console.log("Loading weapons and firing");
      }
}

const phantom = new FighterPlane(2);

phantom.fly();
// Engines on, and the plane is gone

phantom.showCapacity();
// 2
```

If you wish to access the parent class version of the method, you can do so using `super.fly()` as follows:

```
class FighterPlane extends AeroPlane {
      fly() {
            super.fly();
            console.log("Engines on, and the plane is gone");
      }
}
```

This ensures that first, the parent class's method will be called every time the fly()
method is called on the FighterPlane's instance. Besides methods, you can also override
constructors; consider the following code snippet, for example:

```
class AeroPlane {
      constructor(capacity, color) {
            this.capacity = capacity;
            this.color = color;
      }
}
class FighterPlane extends AeroPlane {
      constructor(color) {
            // This fighterplane is 2-seater
            super(2, color);
      }
}

const phantom = new FighterPlane("grey");

console.log(phantom.capacity);        // 2
```

Inheritable Built-Ins

ES6 makes it really easy to inherit from built-in classes like Array, String, RegEx, etc.,
which can be really helpful in cases where you need data structures like stacks, queues, or
any other linked-list structures. You can also utilize this functionality to avail additional
helper methods on arrays like first, last, shuffle, etc., based on your needs.

Consider the following code snippet where we are implementing a ReversedString
data type by extending String built-in class:

```
class ReversedString extends String {

      print() {
            return this.split('').reverse().join('');
      }

}
```

```
const str = new ReversedString("Awesome");

console.log(str.print());
// emosewA
```

Summary

ES6 classes formalize an existing pattern in JavaScript of building pseudo-classes mimicking the class-based development pattern in other programming languages. They make inheritance in JavaScript easier to use and provide you with syntactic sugar to implement the classical prototypal inheritance model of JavaScript with simpler class-based syntax.

In this chapter, we looked at how classes in ES6 use prototypal inheritance under the hood, by defining non-static methods on the class prototype, while all the static methods are defined on the class itself, making all of the class methods non-enumerable. We also learned about the new class-based inheritance syntax that lets you create derived classes from a base class, also allowing you to inherit from built-in classes like Arrays, Strings, and other data types in JavaScript. On the whole, classes are a very important syntax addition to JavaScript, enabling us to declare custom object types in a much cleaner manner by offering a concise syntax.

CHAPTER 5

■ ■ ■

Modules

JavaScript, in its early days, started out as a simple scripting language for the web browser. Hence it was originally built with an approach where *"everything was shared."* But over time, as the language evolved and as JavaScript applications started getting more and more complex, this approach to loading code started to become a lot more error prone and confusing. Contrast this to the fact that most high-level languages use concepts like modules and packages to help with defining code scope. Prior to ES6, everything inside a JavaScript application, including code across different files of the application, shared the same scope. This is where modules come in to help better manage and introduce code separation, reducing problems like naming collisions and increasing data security. JavaScript developers were forced to resort to external libraries to incorporate modules to help with these particular issues, but with ES6, modules have now been included as an official part of the language.

Module Systems and a Little History

In the past, JavaScript has had two major module systems: the Asynchronous Module Definition (AMD) and CommonJS. CommonJS is a commonly implemented module standard in Node.js. It has a concise syntax and is designed for synchronous loading and servers. AMD, on the other hand, is a popular implementation in RequireJS with a slightly more complex syntax that allows it to work without eval() or a step for compilation. It is designed for asynchronous loading and browsers. Both are not natively available in browsers.

When TC39 decided to implement the module spec in ES6, rather than using one of these two, they came up with a new approach for implementing it. Their goal was to cater to both users of CommonJS and AMD. This new approach built upon both of them and tried to solve many of the problems commonly faced by developers in these implementations.

The ES6 modules provide features from both AMD and CommonJS. They use a compact syntax and a static module structure that aids in code optimization, static checking, and eliminating dead code. It also comes with support for cyclic dependencies like in the case of CommonJS and has support for asynchronous loading and configurable module loading like in AMD.

Ending the fragmentation between CommonJS and AMD and having a single native standard for modules brings with it additional advantages such as doing away with the UMD (Universal Module Definition) pattern traditionally used to enable the same file to be used with different systems.

© Deepak Grover and Hanu Kunduru 2017   65
D. Grover and H. P. Kunduru, *ES6 for Humans*, DOI 10.1007/978-1-4842-2623-0_5

The Module Pattern in Traditional JavaScript

To help us better understand Modules before getting into ES6 modules, we will implement the module pattern in traditional JavaScript. Put simply, a module is a function with inner variables and functions, which can then be exposed to an outside environment by returning a "public API," which gives access to the data inside the function via methods that have closures over the data. To illustrate this, let us write a function using the module pattern:

```
function Message(text) {
    function printMessage() {
        console.log("This is the message: " + text + "!");
    }
    return {
        printMessage: printMessage
    };
}

var printer = Message("test");
printer.printMessage();            // This is the message: test!
```

Here in this example, the variable `printer` is assigned a function `Message` with an argument `"test."` `Message` is the function implementing the module pattern, which gives a `printer` a public API with access to its inner function `printMessage` as a method that prints out the `text` parameter.

Modules in ES6

Modules in ES6 make it easier to compartmentalize and separate code into smaller stand-alone snippets that can then be reused and injected into other places as and when they are required, making the process of testing your code easier as the modules are decoupled from the primary code. Modules are also useful in loading scripts asynchronously, improving load times of apps. But module systems are not exactly new to JavaScript.

Modules are simply JavaScript files that are loaded into JavaScript code from other files. But it is important to understand how this differs from the way scripts are loaded. If we consider the semantics of a JavaScript module in comparison to traditional script loading, a few key differences become apparent. First, modules always run in strict mode unlike traditional scripts where it can be changed. If you look at the top-level scope of the module, the value of `this` is `undefined` and the variables created at the top level are not present in the shared global scope. Anything and everything that you need from inside the module has to be explicitly exported for us to be able to use them outside the module. Let us now take a look at the core value of a module by understanding the ability to import and export binding.

Exporting

The 'export' keyword can be used to expose parts of code inside modules to other modules. You can export a variable, a function, or a class declaration from a module. Variables, Functions, or Classes not exported from a module are not accessible outside the module. Let us look at a few examples:

```
export var text = "ES6 is awesome";
export let name = "Ian Murawski";
export const number = 7;
```

Here in this example, you are exporting text, name, and number, all declared using different variable declaration keywords. You can also export a function or a Class from the module. Consider the following examples:

```
export function add(a, b) {
    return a + b;
}

export class Rectangle {
    constructor(length, width) {
        this.length = length;
        this.width = width;
    }
}
```

In this code snippet we are exporting the function add and Class Rectangle. You can also export an existing function that is private to the module as well.

```
function multiply(a, b) {
    return a * b;
}
export { multiply };
```

From this example, we can see that not just a function declaration – but also a reference to a private function of the module – can be exported.

At this point it is important to understand that only functions or class declarations with names can be exported in this way, and all such exports are referred to as *Named Exports*. You cannot export anonymous functions or classes from a module unless they are marked as default *Exports* specified using the default keyword. You can have multiple named exports in a module but only one default export. It is possible to use both at the same time, but usually it is good practice to keep them separate.

Default Exports

In Node.js, it is a common practice to have modules that export only single values. Even in front-end JS where we use classes for models and components, one class per module is a common practice. An ES6 module is built to pick a default export that will be the main exported value.

A single variable, function, or class can be specified as the default export of the module using the default keyword. You can have only one value as a default export inside a module. Using the keyword on more than one export inside the module will raise an error. Default exports help in reducing the syntax for importing exports from a module.

```
export default function(a, b) {
    return a * b;
}
```

In this example, the function is exported from the module as its default. You can notice how the function does not require a name as it is the default, and the module itself represents the function, allowing you to omit the name for the function. You can also assign it a name and export the function name using default. Consider the following example:

```
function multiply(a, b) {
    return a * b;
}

export default multiply;
```

Importing

Once a module with the relevant exports is set up, it can be accessed inside another module by using the import keyword. There are two parts to an import statement: the identifier you're importing and the module from which those identifiers should be imported. This is the statement in its basic form:

```
import { identifier1, identifier2 } from "./moduleFile.js";
```

In the above statement identifier1 and identifier2 are the bindings imported from moduleFile.js.

The module is specified using a string representing the path to the file containing the module after the from keyword. Notice that the list of bindings looks like a destructured object but remember that it is not. Also the bindings are like variables defined using const, that is, you cannot define any other variables using the same name or import another module with the same name.

Using the above syntax, you can import specific bindings from a module as follows,

```
// importing the functions sum and multiply
import { sum, multiply } from "./ moduleFile.js";
console.log(sum(1, 7));              // 8
console.log(multiply(2, 3));         // 6
```

Here, there are two bindings imported from the moduleFile module: sum and multiply can be used just like locally defined identifiers. But let us consider the case where you want to import all the exports available in the module without having to explicitly declare them by name. This can be done using the wildcard * and importing the identifiers as properties of an object.

```
// import everything
import * as example from "./ moduleFile.js";
console.log(example.sum(1,7));          // 8
console.log(example.multiply(2, 3));    // 6
```

In this code, all exported bindings in moduleFile are loaded into an object called example.

All the exports in the module become accessible as properties of the declared object. This creates a new namespace since the object does not exist within the actual module.

It is important to note that irrespective of the number of times the module is imported in the import statements, it will only be executed once. When the import is executed, the module is stored in memory and reused for all subsequent imports. The file storing the module is executed only once.

Importing Default Values

Importing default values from a module is as simple as,

```
import multiply from "./moduleFile.js";
```

This import statement imports the default value from the module. Notice that we do not use any curly braces unlike when we import named exports. The name multiply in this case is local and will be used to refer to the default value imported from the module.

In case of modules that export both default and non-default values, you can import all the bindings using a single statement.

```
export let message = "42 is the answer to the everything.";

export default function(a, b) {
    return a * b;
}

import multiply, { message } from "./moduleFile.js";

console.log(multiply (21, 2));    // 42
console.log(message);            // "42 is the answer to the everything."
```

You need to use a comma to separate the default local name and the non-default identifiers listed inside curly braces. Make sure to always have the default before the non-default values.

Another way to import a default module with a specific local name would be:

```
import { default as multiply, message } from "./moduleFile.js";
```

In this case, just like the previous example, multiply stores the default module exported from moduleFile.js. We will be discussing renaming identifiers using a keyword later in this chapter.

Exporting an Imported Binding

In case you need to re-export a binding that you imported into the module, you can do that using an export statement:

```
import { message } from "./moduleFile.js";
// some javascript code
export message;
```

In this example, we imported the binding message from moduleFile.js and again exported the same binding. You can also do this in one statement instead of two like this,

```
export { multiply } from "./moduleFile.js";
```

Furthermore, you can re-export everything using the wildcard '*' like in the following example:

```
export * from "./moduleFile.js";
```

In the above example, everything from moduleFile.js is exported out of the current module, including the default value.

Renaming Identifiers

In many cases you might not want to use the original name of the imported variable, function, or class because it can cause a conflict with other declarations in the code. ES6 helps you solve this issue by letting you rename exports and imports using the as keyword.

```
function sum(a, b) {
    return a + b;
}

export { sum as add };
```

In this example, sum is the local name of the exported function. But the function is exported as add and needs to be imported in another module using its exported name add.

```
import { add } from "./moduleFIle.js";
```

Similarly, if you want to use a different name when you import the identifier, you can do something like this,

```
import { add as sum } from "./moduleFile.js";
console.log(typeof add);            // "undefined"
console.log(sum(1, 2));             // 3
```

Here, the exported name add is imported as sum. Therefore, technically there is no identifier named add available for use in the rest of the code. It can only be referred to as sum.

You can also rename an identifier to default to make it a default export.

```
function multiply(a, b) {
    return a * b;
}

export { multiply as default };
```

Similarly, as we discussed before, you can import defaults after renaming them as well:

```
import { default as multiply, message } from "moduleFile.js";

console.log(multiply(1, 2));        // 2
console.log(message);               // "42 is the answer to the everything."
```

Since default is a keyword in JavaScript, it cannot otherwise be used as a variable, function, or class name. Hence, the use of default to rename an export can be considered a special case to create a consistency with how non-default exports are defined. This syntax is useful if you want to use a single export statement to specify multiple exports, including the default, at once.

Loading Modules

ES6 does not specifically define how to load modules. This is because one of the design goals for the module specification was to remain agnostic to the environment where it is implemented. Instead of creating a specification that would work on all JavaScript environments, ES6 only specifies the syntax. Browsers and Node.js need to decide how to implement the HostResolveImportedModule, which is the internal operation to which ES6 abstracts the loading mechanism.

Modules in Web Browsers

There are many ways of using JavaScript inside your web applications but the primary way of inserting JavaScript inside html is through the <script> tag. The <script> tag has an src attribute letting you inform the application that the script is at a particular location. Another way is to directly include code inside the tag. You can also use workers to load JavaScript. Let us look at each of these mechanisms in the context of modules.

Loading Modules with <script>

The <script> element loads JavaScript files as scripts by default. It is equivalent to explicitly mentioning the type attribute with the content type as "text/javascript". In order to support modules, the value module was added to type options. For example,

```
<script type="module" src="moduleFile.js"></script>
<!-- load JavaScript file and recognize it as a module-->

<script type="module">
<!–an inline module -->

import { multiply } from "./moduleFile.js";
let result = multiply(1, 2);
</script>
```

Unlike scripts, modules use import to specify other files that need to be loaded for it to execute correctly. For this functionality to work properly, the module type for the script element always behaves as if the defer attribute was applied. The defer attribute is optional for loading script files but is always applied for loading module files. The module file starts getting downloaded as soon as the HTML parser encounters a `<script type="module">` element. So all modules are executed in the order in which they appear.

Loading Modules Asynchronously in Browsers

You might have already used the async attribute of the `<script>` tag in html. When you use this attribute inside the script tag, it lets the browser know that the script needs to be executed as soon as it has been fetched and is available. Therefore the order in which async scripts are executed is not synchronous. They are executed as soon as they are available, whichever order they might have been declared. You can use the same asynchronous process of execution when it comes to modules. The only small thing to keep in mind is that the import resources need to be fetched first before the module can be executed.

Common Pitfalls

Modules can be extremely useful in compartmentalizing code and creating reusable logical components. But there are a few pitfalls you should be aware of to use them effectively. In this section, we will be discussing these pitfalls in detail.

Syntax

Remember that both export and import need to be used only at the top level and cannot be part of other statements or functions. For example, the following code will throw a syntax error.

```
if (condition) {
    export condition;
    // SyntaxError: 'import' and 'export' may only appear at the top level
}
```

Here, the export statement is part of an if statement, which throws an error. Exports and imports cannot be executed conditionally or dynamically in any way. This also stands true in case of using import-export statements in a try-catch block. The export and import keywords were specifically designed to be static so that text-editors could easily provide the information that is available from a specific module when it is imported.

Read-Only Bindings

ES6 import statements only produce read-only bindings to the corresponding variables, functions, or classes. Therefore, the module that imports them cannot change its value. But the module that exports an identifier can make changes to it. For example,

```
// moduleFile.js    starts here
export var message = "Message from moduleFile";

export function setMessage(newText) {
    message = newText;
}
// moduleFile.js    ends here

// file.js
import { message, setMessage } from "./moduleFile.js"
console.log(message);              // "Message from moduleFile"

setMessage ("New Message");
console.log(message);              // "New Message"

message = "This is another message";      // error
```

In the above example, we import two bindings from the module, message and setMessage. The function setMessage() can change the value of the variable message but when you try to directly change the value it throws an error.

Destructing an Import Statement and Using Variables

Even though the import statement looks like destructuring, it is not. Hence, the following code is invalid and will throw an error.

```
import { toto: { tata } } from 'someModule'; //error
```

You have to also keep in mind that an import statement should not depend on anything that needs to be computed during runtime. Therefore, something like the following example will also throw an error.

```
import toto from "someModule" + tata; //error
```

Hence, try and make sure not to use any such complicated mechanisms while importing from a module.

Using eval()

You cannot use eval() on modules since they are a high-level construct for it. Eval() usually accepts scripts that do not allow import or export.

Module Specifier

In all of the examples above, we used a relative path in the module specifier like "./moduleFile.js". When browsers try to run this code, they understand them in the following manner:

- / resolves to the root directory
- ./ resolves to the current directory
- ./ resolves to the parent directory

Summary

Modules in ES6 provide new ways to extend the functionality of JavaScript. They help in better organizing code and maintaining a more modular semantic code base. ES6 introduces new keywords like import, export, and default to make the use of modules possible. You no longer need to use UMD or additional modules systems like CommonJS or AMD as ES6 brings in the best of both worlds.

Using modules you can write reusable and better packaged code. Modules do not modify the global scope, unlike scripts, giving you a lesser chance for error. You have to specifically export all the values out of the module if you want to use them elsewhere.

CHAPTER 6

Symbols in ES6

Since way back in 1996, around the time when JavaScript was first standardized and
ECMA attempted to carve out a standard specification, there have been five primitive
data types in JavaScript: Boolean, Number, String, Undefined, and Null where each type
represents a value. But now ES6 introduces a brand new primitive data type - Symbol. In
this chapter, we will go over, in detail, this new primitive type and its applications.

Symbols

Symbols represent a unique value and at its heart, a symbol is a unique token that is
guaranteed to never clash with any other Symbol. Symbols in ES6 can be created using a
factory function. The Symbol() method can be used to create a new symbol. Consider the
following example:

```
const foo = Symbol();
console.log(typeof foo);        // "symbol"
```

Every time you call the factory function, a new and unique symbol is created. The
output from the typeof on a symbol type is "symbol," and this is the primary way to
identify symbols:

■ **Note**   Symbols in ES6 do not have a literal form like other primitives.

Optionally, while creating a Symbol you can also give it a label by passing a string as
an argument into the Symbol() method:

```
const chocolate = Symbol("this is my chocolate");

console.log(chocolate);
// Symbol(this is my chocolate)

console.log(chocolate.toString());
// "Symbol(this is my chocolate)"
```

The label passed in as the argument does not affect the value of the Symbol. It has no other consequence except for being a string to describe the symbol while printing it. It is also useful when you call .toString() method on the returned symbol, which converts the symbol into a string. This label is shown when you write the symbol to console.log(), and possibly in error messages. This can be helpful for debugging purposes.

Note that you should not be using the new keyword for creating symbols. Symbols do not have an object constructor; therefore you cannot create a Symbol using the new keyword:

```
const bar = new Symbol();          // Type Error
```

As mentioned before, a symbol is always unique and two symbols can never be the same. You can, however, create multiple symbols with the same label but the returned symbols would always be unique. Check the following code snippet for an example:

```
const kit = Symbol("hello");
const kat = Symbol("hello");

console.log(kit === kat);     // false
```

or you can simply try,

```
Symbol() !== Symbol()        // true
```

Hence, symbols are always unique and can be of incredible use in various cases. Let's take a look at their applications in the next section.

Applications of Symbols

Symbols, by their very nature, are mainly used as unique property keys because a symbol can never clash with any other property (symbol or string) of the object, which can be incredibly helpful in cases where you don't want to take chances on overriding native properties of an object. Symbols are also commonly used to create anonymous (or private in some sense) properties for the internal use of a class or an object type. Consider the following example, where we have an object Person with some "public" properties:

```
let Person = {
        name: "John",
        age: 14,
        location: "New York"
}
```

Now let's suppose we want to add a private method to the Person object. We can do that using Symbols as follows:

```
let votingEligibility = Symbol();
Person[votingEligibility] = function() {
        return this.age >= 18;
}
```

Let's look at the Person object now, and you can see that an anonymous method has been added to it.

```
console.log(Person);
// {name: "John", age: 14, location: "New York"}

// If you are running this in a recent version of Google Chrome,
// you will see - Symbol(): [Function]  property as well
```

You can also use computed property keys here, which we have already discussed in a previous chapter:

```
let Person = {
        name: "John",
        age: 14,
        location: "New York",
        [Symbol()]: function() {
                return this.age >= 18;
        }
}
```

The Symbol property is non-enumerable and anonymous. Therefore, when using the for...in loop, symbol properties of the object won't be accessible while traversing, and since it is anonymous, it will not be listed in the resultant array of Object. getOwnPropertyNames() method. However, you can get the Symbol property using Object.getOwnPropertySymbols(). For example:

```
Object.getOwnPropertyNames(Person);
// ["name", "age", "location"]

Object.getOwnPropertySymbols(Person);
// [Symbol()]
```

Let us take a look at how you would use Object.getOwnPropertySymbols() in the previous example where we created the Person object.

```
let canVote = Object.getOwnPropertySymbols(Person)[0];

Person[canVote]();

// false
```

■ **Note**   We saw that Object.getOwnPropertySymbols() returns an array of Property Symbols associated with an object, hence these properties are accessible and not private. But using symbols, we definitely have the advantage of not discovering these properties casually.

You can also achieve this by using the reference created to bind the property with the Person object. Remember how we created the symbol using let votingEligibility = Symbol();. Therefore,

```
Person[votingEligibility]();
// false
```

Similarly, custom classes can also create private members this way, making them available privately to the other methods defined in the class. The dynamically created symbol value can be saved to a scoped class variable that can be accessed only by the internal methods of the class, shielding the private properties from unwanted and casual discovery. Consider the following code snippet, for example:

```
const age = Symbol("age");

class Person {
        constructor(value) {
                this[age] = value;
        }

        getAge() {
                console.log(this[age]);
        }
}

const jack = new Person(23);

console.log(jack);
// Person {}

console.log(jack.age);
// undefined

console.log(jack[Symbol("age")]);
// undefined

jack.getAge();
// 23
```

In this example, we have a Person class that creates a private property using Symbols to store the age of the person. As apparent from the code snippet, the property is non-enumerable since it returns an empty object and can only be accessed via the exposed getAge() method. Since Symbols are always unique, accessing the private property by creating the symbol with the same label age: Symbol("age") will only create a new unique symbol, and it will not be able to access the desired property of the object.

Symbols and Registry

So far, we have talked about local symbols and how you can access them by obtaining a reference. Symbols can also be placed in a global registry, from where they can be accessed across different contexts known as realms. A realm is a context in which pieces of code exist such as the page your application is running in, or an <iframe> within your page, or a web worker with their context containing global variables and loaded modules.

Symbols come with a special power to be available throughout the runtime-wide symbol registry, and you can use the following methods to add symbols to the runtime-wide symbol registry:

```
Symbol.for(key) and Symbol.keyFor(symbol).
```

Symbol.for(key)

This method looks up existing symbols in the runtime-wide symbol registry with the given key. If a symbol with that key exists in the global registry, that symbol is returned. If no symbol with that key is found in the registry, a new symbol gets created. Consider the following code snippet, for example, where the first call to Symbol.for('myCar') creates a symbol, adds it to the registry, and returns it; and the second call returns that same symbol because the key is already in the runtime-wide symbol registry:

```
Symbol.for('myCar') === Symbol.for('myCar')
// true
```

The runtime global registry keeps track of all the symbols created using Symbol.for(key) method, which can be accessed across different realms. For instance, a symbol created anywhere in your webpage can be accessed in an iframe's context as well. Check the following code snippet (you can run this in your browser's console):

```
// create an iframe
const frame = document.createElement('iframe');

// append the iframe to body
document.body.appendChild(frame);

console.log(Symbol.for('temperature') === frame.contentWindow.Symbol.
for('temperature'));
// true
```

In the above example, Global Symbol from the webpage's context is identical to the Global Symbol in the iframe, which tells us that the symbols created using Symbol.for(key) method can be accessed across different realms.

Symbol.keyFor(symbol)

Symbol.keyFor(symbol) retrieves the key from the global symbol registry that was associated with the given symbol when the symbol was added to the registry. It returns undefined when the symbol is not found in the registry.

```
const symbol = Symbol.for('myHouse');

console.log(Symbol.keyFor(symbol)); // myHouse

const myCat = Symbol();

Symbol.keyFor(myCat); // undefined
```

Built-In Symbols

ES6 comes with a range of symbols that are predefined in the language specification, most of which expose some meta properties and behaviors of JavaScript objects. Some of the well-known symbols are the following:

Symbol.hasInstance - which allows us to determine whether an object is the instance of the constructor. It is called by instanceof operator internally.

Another one is Symbol.iterator that we will be digging into later in this book. It holds the default iterator of an object. Arrays, Sets, Maps, and WeakMaps have a non-enumerable [Symbol.iterator] property present in their structure.

Summary

Symbols are a new primitive type introduced to JavaScript in ES6. They can be incredibly helpful when you want to avoid name clashes in property keys, especially in cases where you don't want to take chances on overriding native properties of an object. Symbols, being non-enumerable, provide an advantage by creating protected properties, preventing them from being discovered casually as you have to specifically look for symbols to find them.

CHAPTER 7

■ ■ ■

Arrays and Collections

Up until this point, we have covered many new and improved features and functionalities that ES6 offers. In this chapter, we will look at a few more enhancements to data types like arrays and collections. ES6 brings to the JavaScript language many new static properties and methods that extend the functionality of built-in natives and objects. We will take a look at the extended features of the Array type and some of the new data structure abstractions that are now native components of the language.

Arrays and New Methods

Over the years, many popular JavaScript libraries like Underscore and Lodash have evolved with the array data structure being one of the most commonly extended features. Therefore, over time it had become increasingly necessary to have built-in support in the language for a range of array functionalities made common by these libraries. In this section, we will introduce all the new ES6 array functionalities and look into a few use cases where they shine.

We now have a few new static and prototype methods that the language offers to help you create, manipulate, fill, and filter arrays. First let's take a look at the static methods: `Array.from()` and `Array.of()`, and then we will explore the new prototype methods introduced for Arrays in ES6.

Array.from()

Prior to ES6, in order to convert the array-like objects (e.g., `arguments` and `NodeList`) to a true array, we needed to use hacks like calling `Array.prototype.slice.call()` on the `arguments` or `NodeList` to convert the objects into arrays. Consider the following example, where you have a list of elements present in the DOM:

```
<ul>
        <li>Apple</li>
        <li>Mango</li>
        <li>Orange</li>
        <li>Litchi</li>
        <li>Banana</li>
</ul>
```

© Deepak Grover and Hanu Kunduru 2017
D. Grover and H. P. Kunduru, *ES6 for Humans*, DOI 10.1007/978-1-4842-2623-0_7

```
var listItems = document.querySelectorAll('li');

// converting NodeList to an array
listItems = Array.prototype.slice.call(listItems);

// using Array methods on the newly converted array
listItems.map(item => { console.log(item.innerText) });

// Apple
// Mango
// Orange
// Litchi
// Banana
```

With ES6, we now have a more straightforward solution for converting array-like objects like the ones described in the above example, into arrays. The new `Array.from` static method allows us to create arrays from any array-like or iterable objects. Before we move forward though, let's clearly understand what we actually mean by array-like objects. These are simply the objects that have a length property or indexed elements. For example, consider the following object:

```
const customers = {
    '0': 'matt',
    '1': 'ian',
    '2': 'mikhail',
    '3': 'akia',
    '4': 'vincent',
    length: 5
};
```

Now, if we were to convert this object into an array, we can do it using the Array. from() syntax simply like this:

```
Array.from(customers).forEach(customer => {
    console.log(customer);
});
```

In this example, we just passed into the function the customer object, and in turn it returns an array formed from the individual elements. Let's look at the specific Array.from syntax:

```
Array.from(arrayLike[, mapFn[, thisArg]])
```

In this syntax **arrayLike** is an array-like or iterable object and **mapFn,** which is an optional argument is a Map function that can be applied on every element of the array. **thisArg** is another optional argument whose value is used as this when executing the mapFn.

Array.from() tries to check if its first argument is an iterable, and if it is it uses the iterator to produce values to copy into the returned array. But if you pass an array-like object, it behaves the same as slice() or apply() does, which is simply loop over the values accessing numerically names properties from 0 to the length of the object.

If we now use the above example with the optional mapFn argument, it would look like this:

```
Array.from(customers, customer => {
    console.log(customer);
});
```

Notice how we have removed the forEach method and used a second argument as a map function to iterate over the resultant array.

Array.of()

Another really handy method introduced in ES6 is Array.of(), which lets you create an array of elements easily. Array.of() takes a list of items as parameters and returns them to you as an array. Consider the following example,

```
let arr = Array.of(10, 20, 30, 40);
console.log(arr); // [10, 20, 30, 40]
```

You might be wondering how is this different from the traditional Array(...) constructor. You can also create an array with the array constructor method using the Array() syntax. But, the difference between Array.of() and the Array constructor is the way they handle a single number as an argument. The Array constructor has a very weird behavior where if only one number is passed to it, instead of making an array of one element with that number value, it constructs an empty array with the number as its length. All the elements are set to undefined.

The Array.of() static method fixes this issue and is now the preferred function-form constructor for arrays.

Take a look at the following example:

```
const arr1 = Array.of(10);
console.log(arr1); // [10]
console.log(arr1.length);     // 1

const arr2 = Array(10);
console.log(arr2); // [,,,,,,,,,]
console.log(arr2.length);     // 10
```

As you can see in the example above, the Array.of(10) creates an array of single number [10], whereas new Array(10) method creates an empty array of length 10. All that said and done, we need to understand why we would have to use the constructor in the first place instead of a literal syntax like a = [1, 2, 3]. You would use the constructor, for example, in case you have a callback that is supposed to wrap arguments passed to it into an array or if you have to subclass Array and want to create or initialize elements in an instance of your subclass.

Now that we have looked at the two new static methods introduced for Arrays in ES6, let's dig deeper into the new prototype methods introduced for the Array prototype in ES6.

New Array.Prototype Methods

Now that we have discussed the new methods to create arrays, let's take a look at how the new array methods introduced in ES6 help us access and manipulate data stored in the arrays easily. In this section, we will go over the new Array.prototype methods, which include entries(), keys(), values(), find(), findIndex(), fill(), and copyWithin(), and see some practical examples to understand how these methods help us access and manipulate data easily.

Array.prototype.entries( )

The entries() method returns a sequence of values, but reveals them one by one using an iterator, instead of all at once as an array. You will learn about iterators in greater detail in a later chapter, but let's have a quick introduction to iterators here.

An iterator accesses the items from a collection one at a time, while keeping track of its current position within that sequence. It provides a next() method that returns the next item in the sequence. The next() method returns an object with two properties: done and value, where value represents the item in the collection and done is a Boolean that is true when all the elements of the iterable have been iterated over.

Every iterable (e.g., array) must implement the *iterable protocol*, meaning that the object (or one of the objects up its prototype chain) must have a property with a Symbol. iterator key. Symbol.iterator is another ES6 addition that we will discuss later in this book, but for now, think of this as a way to define special keys that will never conflict with regular object keys.

Let's look at an array, which is an iterable, and the iterator it can produce to consume its values:

```
const arr = [11,12,13];
const itr = arr[Symbol.iterator]();

itr.next(); // { value: 11, done: false }
itr.next(); // { value: 12, done: false }
itr.next(); // { value: 13, done: false }

itr.next(); // { value: undefined, done: true }
```

Now that we have a basic understanding of iterators and iterables, let's take a good look at how the Array.prototype.entries() method helps us iterate over an array. This method returns a new Array Iterator object that contains the key/value pairs for each index in the array. Consider the following code snippet, for example:

```
const breakfast = ['apples', 'bananas', 'oranges'];
const eBreakfast = breakfast.entries();

console.log(eBreakfast.next().value); // [0, 'apples']
console.log(eBreakfast.next().value); // [1, 'bananas']
console.log(eBreakfast.next().value); // [2, 'oranges']
```

You can also use a for-of loop to iterate over the iterator returned from the breakfast.entries() call:

```
for (let entry of eBreakfast) {
    console.log(entry);
}

// [0, 'apples']
// [1, 'bananas']
// [2, 'oranges']
```

Similarly, there are two more array methods to access the keys and values separately. Let's take a look at them.

Array.prototype.keys( )

This method returns a new Array Iterator that contains the keys for each index in the array:

```
const breakfast = ['apples', 'bananas', 'oranges'];
const kBreakfast = breakfast.keys();

console.log(kBreakfast.next().value); // 0
console.log(kBreakfast.next().value); // 1
console.log(kBreakfast.next().value); // 2
```

Array.prototype.values( )

This method returns a new Array Iterator object that contains the values for each index in the array:

```
const breakfast = ['apples', 'bananas', 'oranges'];
const vBreakfast = breakfast.values();

console.log(vBreakfast.next().value); // apples
console.log(vBreakfast.next().value); // bananas
console.log(vBreakfast.next().value); // oranges
```

Array.prototype.find( )

The find() method lets you iterate through your array and returns the first item that matches the callback(element, index, array) for the array. This method also allows you to optionally pass a context binding for this. In other words, the find() method returns the first value in the array for which the testing function returns true; otherwise undefined is returned. The syntax for the find() method looks like this:

```
arr.find(callback[, thisArg])
```

where callback is the testing function that is executed on each value and takes three arguments:

element, index and array.

```
function callback(element, index, array) {
// returns true or false based on some condition
}
```

Consider the following code snippet:

```
const inventory = [
    {name: 'apples', quantity: 2},
    {name: 'bananas', quantity: 0},
    {name: 'oranges', quantity: 5}
];

let result = inventory.find((fruit) => fruit.name === 'apples');
console.log(result);              // {name: 'apples', quantity: 2}
```

The above example shows how we can easily find the first element that matches the fruit.name as 'apples' in the given array. You can also use find() method to get the element at a certain index position, for example:

```
result = inventory.find((fruit, i) => i > 2);
console.log(result);              // {name: 'oranges', quantity: 5}
```

As mentioned above, the find() method returns undefined if the element is not found in the array:

```
result = inventory.find((fruit, i) => i > 10);
console.log(result);             // undefined
```

The next argument thisArg lets you optionally pass a context binding for this; for example, consider the following code snippet:

```
function eligibleToVote(age) {
    return age >= this.legalAge;
}
```

```
function foo() {
    this.legalAge = 18;
    const result = [10, 12, 23, 26, 32].find(eligibleToVote, this);
    console.log(result);
}

foo();     // 23
```

In this example, the context of foo is passed as the second argument in the find() method, due to which this in eligibleToVote() refers to the context of foo and this. legalAge is 18.

You might think that this method is similar to filter() method from ES5, but note that filter() always returns an array of matches (and will return multiple matches), whereas find() always returns only one element (first one in the array that matches the condition).

Array.prototype.findIndex( )

This method is an equivalent of find(). Instead of returning an item, this method returns the index position. If none of the elements in the collection match the callback (element, index, array) criteria, the return value is -1.

Consider the following code snippet, for example:

```
result = inventory.findIndex((fruit) => fruit.name === 'apples');

console.log(result);                    // 0
result = inventory.findIndex((fruit) => fruit.name === 'grapes');

console.log(result);                    // -1
```

This method is similar to the indexOf()method from ES5, which simply locates the element in the array. With the indexOf() method, you can only search for an element inside an array; it doesn't support a callback method. Whereas in case of the findIndex()method, we have the capability to apply a condition to which the element at the returned index position must satisfy.

Array.prototype.fill( )

This is a very simple method that allows us to fill all the elements of an array with a static value. It also takes optional start and end index values.

Consider the following code snippet:

```
[1, 2, 3].fill(4);          // [4, 4, 4]
[1, 2, 3].fill(4, 1);       // [1, 4, 4]
[1, 2, 3].fill(4, 1, 2);    // [1, 4, 3]
```

The input value can be arbitrary, not necessarily a number, character, or any other primitive type. It can be an object, for example:

```
new Array(4).fill({});      // [{}, {}, {}]
```

Array.prototype.copyWithin( )

The copyWithin()method copies the sequence of array elements within the array to the position starting at target. The elements that should be copied are taken from the (start, end) range. The start argument is optional and defaults to 0. Also, the end argument is also optional and defaults to the length of the array.

The syntax of copyWithin() method looks like this:

```
Array.prototype.copyWithin(target, start = 0, end = this.length)
```

Let's start with a simple example. Consider the following code snippet:

```
let fruits = ["apples", "bananas", "oranges", "grapes", "guava",
"watermelon"];

fruits.copyWithin(4);

console.log(fruits);
// ["apples", "bananas", "oranges", "grapes", "apples", "bananas"]
```

fruits.copyWithin(4) considers the target index at 4, which is "guava." It further determines the items to be copied will be taken as start at 0 (default) and end at 6 (length of the array). You can obviously specify start and end values as per your needs:

```
fruits = ["apples", "bananas", "oranges", "grapes", "guava", "watermelon"];

fruits.copyWithin(4, 1, 3);

console.log(fruits);
// ["apples", "bananas", "oranges", "grapes", "bananas", "oranges"]
```

The copyWithin() method also accepts negative start indices, negative end indices, and negative target indices. Let's look at an example using that:

```
[1, 2, 3, 4, 5].copyWithin(-3, -4, -1);     // [1, 2, 2, 3, 4]
```

In this example, -3 as the target index determines the start position as the third element from the last of the array (which is 3 in the input array). It further determines the start and end values as 2 and 5 (the fourth and first element from the end of the array), respectively.

Typed Arrays

Typed arrays in ES6 provide an efficient way for accessing and manipulating binary data. Before ES6, JavaScript was not very good at handling binary data. Typed arrays help in improving the performance when it comes to handling binary data.

With typed arrays, JavaScript engines do not have to deduce the type of the array. If you make an ordinary array in JavaScript, and only store floating-point numbers in it, your JavaScript engine may optimistically decide that it's an array of floating-point numbers and optimize the code for it. The performance can then be equivalent to that of typed arrays. But, let's consider a case where you have an array of floating-point numbers and at some point in your code, you store an object in an element. In this case, your JavaScript engine has to de-optimize and regenerate code that makes the array generic again. Therefore, with Typed arrays, things are much simpler as they're guaranteed to be one type, and you just can't store other things like objects in them. The fact they're much simpler means that less-sophisticated JavaScript engines can easily implement them, and you can achieve a consistent performance throughout.

The architecture of a typed array is comprised of a buffer and a view. A buffer is an object that represents a chunk of data. We can't directly manipulate the contents of a buffer. In order to access the memory contained in the buffer, we need to use a view. A view enables us to read and write the data content of the buffer.

So, typed arrays have two separate classes: ArrayBuffer and DataView. The ArrayBuffer contains our data and the DataView provides a custom view into this data, which represents the buffer in a specific format and enables data access and manipulation.

Basics of Using Typed Arrays

Check the following code snippet; here we are creating an ArrayBuffer and then a specific DataView to handle the data inside that buffer:

```
const buffer = new ArrayBuffer(16);
const int32View = new Int32Array(buffer);

for (let i = 0; i < int32View.length; i++) {
    int32View[i] = i * 2;
}

console.log(int32View); // [0, 2, 4, 6]
```

Typed array views provide views for all the usual numeric types like Int8, Uint32, Float64, etc. You can check all the types and their respective size and description in Table 7-1.

Table 7-1. Typed array views

Type	Size in bytes	Description
Int8Array	1	8-bit signed integer
Uint8Array	1	8-bit unsigned integer
Uint8ClampedArray	1	8-bit unsigned integer (clamped)
Int16Array	2	16-bit signed integer
Uint16Array	2	16-bit unsigned integer
Int32Array	4	32-bit signed integer
Uint32Array	4	32-bit unsigned integer
Float32Array	4	32-bit floating-point number
Float64Array	8	64-bit floating-point number

Note that in case of clamped arrays, all values outside the range are set to the nearest element in the range, that is, the first or last element. The Uint8ClampedArray typed array represents an array of 8-bit unsigned integers clamped to 0-255, which means if you specify a value that is out of the range of [0,255], 0 or 255 will be set instead. If you specify a non-integer, the nearest integer will be set.

Typed Arrays and Normal Arrays

Typed arrays and Normal arrays are similar in some ways: they both have length property, and in the both of the cases, elements in the array can be accessed using the [ ] operator. Typed arrays also support all standard array methods. But they do differ in various ways.

Typed arrays in JavaScript are similar to arrays in other programming languages like C, C++ where all the elements of an array are of the same type, unlike arrays in JavaScript where elements can be of any type. Typed arrays have a strict type for all the elements.

Typed arrays cannot have empty elements. They are always initialized with a 0 value, unlike normal arrays where values can be empty (undefined). Check the following code snippet:

```
const buffer = new ArrayBuffer(16);
const float32View = new Float32Array(buffer);
let arr = new Array(10);

console.log(float32View); // Float32Array [0, 0, 0, 0]
console.log(arr); // [,,,,,,,,,,]
```

Typed arrays are supported by various browser APIs: File API, XMLHttpRequest, Fetch API, Canvas, WebSockets, WebGL, Web Audio API, Media elements, etc. Currently, some of the features of Typed Arrays might not be supported by all the browsers and JavaScript engines, so you can check the availability for the desired JavaScript engine at https://kangax.github.io/compat-table/es6/#typed_arrays.

Map and WeakMap

ES6 introduces a new set of data structures called Map and WeakMap, which are fundamentally a hash table or a dictionary as referred in Python or C#. ES6 Maps provide a simple API to store objects by an arbitrary key, a pretty essential functionality required in many JavaScript programs. We will go into details about each of them in this section.

Map

We actually use maps in JavaScript all the time. In fact, every object can be considered a Map. An object is made of keys (always strings) and values, whereas in Map, any value (both objects and primitive values) can be used as either a key or a value.

In Map, keys can be of any type: string, Boolean, number, object, or function. Have a look at this piece of code:

```
let myMap = new Map();

const keyString = "a string",
keyObj = {},
        keyFunc = () => {};

// setting the values

myMap.set(keyString, "value associated with 'a string'");
myMap.set(keyObj, "value associated with keyObj");
myMap.set(keyFunc, "value associated with keyFunc");
```

Note that the set() method is chainable so you can alternatively do this:

```
myMap.set(keyString, "value associated with 'a string'")
.set(keyObj, "value associated with keyObj")
.set(keyFunc, "value associated with keyFunc");

myMap.size; // 3

// getting the values
myMap.get(keyString);    // "value associated with 'a string'"
myMap.get(keyObj);       // "value associated with keyObj"
myMap.get(keyFunc);      // "value associated with keyFunc"
```

Checking Keys Equality

Key equality in Map() is based on the "same-value" algorithm, which is similar to the === operator but also considers NaN to be equal to NaN (even though generally NaN !== NaN), which means NaN when used as a key will return map objects that were previously set using NaN as the key. Consider the following code snippet, for example:

```
let myMap = new Map();

myMap.set(NaN, "not a number");

myMap.get(NaN); // "not a number"
```

Note that you can also create a map via an iterable over key/value pairs:

```
let myMap = new Map([
[ 1, 'apple' ],
      [ 2, 'banana' ],
      [ 3, 'orange' ]
]);
```

Also, maps can be iterated over using for...of or forEach():

```
for (let [key, value] of myMap) {
console.log(key + " = " + value);
}

// 1 = apple
// 2 = banana
// 3 = orange
```

Maps also support keys(), values(), and entries() methods:

```
for (let key of myMap.keys()) {
console.log(key);
}
// 1
// 2
// 3

for (let value of myMap.values()) {
console.log(value);
}
// apple
// banana
// orange
```

```
for (let [key, value] of myMap.entries()) {
console.log(key + " = " + value);
}
// 1 = apple
// 2 = banana
// 3 = orange
```

If you are a seasoned JS developer, you know that objects are the primary mechanism for creating unordered key/value pairs as data structures. However, using objects as maps does not give us the ability to use a non-string value as a key.

At this point, you must be wondering, when and when not to use maps over objects. You should always use a Map when you need a key/value collection, because objects inherently were not designed to be used as collections, and as a result there's no efficient way to determine the number of properties an object has. When you loop over an object's properties, you also get its prototype properties. Of course there are some workarounds for this but when you loop over an object's properties, the properties won't necessarily be retrieved in the same order they were inserted. That's why it is recommended to use maps when you need a key/value collection in your JavaScript program.

A good indicator would also be the case where you don't know the keys of the collection beforehand, that is, they are being read from the database or input by the user, which means they don't necessarily have to be a string or a number. In contrast, you should be using objects when you know which and how many properties the object has while writing the code, that is, when their shape is static.

WeakMap

WeakMaps are similar to normal Maps, albeit with fewer methods and some differences with regards to garbage collection. A WeakMap is a Map in which the keys are weakly referenced, which means a WeakMap doesn't prevent its keys from being garbage collected if all references to the key are lost and there are no more references to the value. Therefore, you don't have to worry about memory leaks with WeakMaps. Usually you want this behavior when storing metadata related to something like a DOM node such that DOM elements should be released from memory when they're no longer of interest.

The biggest limitation in a WeakMap is that it is not iterable, as opposed to Map – which means it does not support entries(), keys(), values(), forEach(), and clear() methods. Another thing to note here is that, in WeakMap, as opposed to a Map, every key **must** be an object.

Although it has almost the same API like a Map, we can't iterate over the WeakMap collection. We can't even determine the length of the collection because we don't have a size attribute here. A WeakMap only has four methods:

- delete(key)
- has(key)
- get(key)
- set(key, value)

```
let wMap = new WeakMap();

wMap.set('a', 'b');
// Uncaught TypeError: Invalid value used as weak map key

const o1 = {},
      o2 = () => {},
      o3 = window;

wMap.set(o1, 42);
wMap.set(o2, "hello");
wMap.set(o3, undefined);

wMap.get(o3); // undefined, because that is the set value
wMap.has(o1); // true
wMap.delete(o1);
wMap.has(o1); // false
```

Set and WeakSet

Sets and WeakSets are yet another collection type introduced in ES6. If you come from programming languages like Python, you would know how incredibly helpful sets can be. Let's take a look at them in this section.

Set

Set objects are collections of unique values. Duplicate values are ignored, as the collection must have all unique values. Sets are fast and the values can be primitive types or object references.

Check the following code snippet to know more about sets and its methods:

```
let mySet = new Set([1, 1, 2, 2, 3, 3]);

mySet.size; // 3

mySet.has(1); // true

mySet.add('strings');
mySet.delete('strings'); // true
mySet.has('strings'); // false

mySet.add({ a: 1, b:2 });

mySet.size; // 4
mySet.clear(); // Clears the set
mySet.size; // 0
```

Note that similar to maps, NaN equals NaN when it comes to Set, too. You can iterate over a set by insertion order using either the forEach method or the for...of loop:

```
mySet = new Set([1, 1, 2, 2, 3, 3, { a: 1, b:2 }]);

mySet.forEach((item) => {
    console.log(item);
});

// 1
// 2
// 3
// Object { a: 1, b: 2 }

for (let value of mySet) {
    console.log(value);
}

// 1
// 2
// 3
// Object { a: 1, b: 2 }
```

Sets can be incredibly helpful if you need a dynamic list of unique elements to be rendered in a drop-down or as an auto-suggestion for an input field. Using Set would ensure that your list of suggestions would never have a duplicate value and saves you the trouble of checking for duplicates.

WeakSet

Similar to WeakMap, the WeakSet object lets you store weakly held objects in a collection, which means a WeakSet doesn't prevent its elements from being garbage collected. An object in the WeakSet occurs only once; it is unique in the WeakSet's collection.

Values in a WeakMap must be unique object references. If nothing else is referencing the object present in a WeakSet, it'll be subject to garbage collection.

Much like a WeakMap, a WeakSet is not iterable and does not have a size property. A WeakSet supports only three methods:

- add(value)

- has(value)

- delete(value)

```
let ws = new WeakSet();
const obj = {};
const foo = {};
```

```
ws.add(window);
ws.add(obj);

ws.has(window); // true
ws.has(foo);    // false, foo has not been added to the set

ws.delete(window); // removes window from the set
ws.has(window);    // false, window has been removed
```

You should use a WeakSet over a Set when you need Garbage Collection capabilities in the collection. Another typical use case would be marking an object as satisfying some or other quality. Consider the following example:

```
const fruits = new WeakSet();

class Fruit {
  constructor() {
    fruits.add(this);
  }

  getName() {
    if (!fruits.has(this)) {
      throw new TypeError("getName() called on an incompatible object!");
    } else {
      // returns the name
    }
  }
}
```

This is a good way to prevent the usage of class methods on any object that was not created by the class constructor.

Summary

In this chapter, we learned the new and effective methods introduced in ES6 to handle and manipulate data using Arrays and Collections. These new features provide built-in solutions for common use cases that were cumbersome prior to ES6. With new Array methods, you have the capabilities to create and manage arrays easily in your JavaScript programs. We also learned about the new array prototype methods introduced in ES6, which help us iterate and access the elements stored in an array efficiently. We also discussed how Typed Arrays help you improve performance when it comes to handling binary data in JavaScript. In the latter half of this chapter, we learned about the new collection types: Maps, WeakMaps, Sets, and WeakSets, introduced in ES6 with their rock solid feature set and effective use cases.

At this point, you should feel confident about using these new data types in your JavaScript applications. In the next chapter, we will be digging into details about briefly discussed iterators and iterables, and learning the concept of generators introduced in ES6.

CHAPTER 8

■ ■ ■

Iterators and Generators

In this chapter, we will be learning all about the newly introduced iterators and generators, which bring simplicity and customizability to the traversing mechanism in JavaScript. A lot of programming languages have already moved away from the boring old for loops that required additional efforts to keep track of the current index position while traversing through the items in the collection. Let's take a look at how we can use iterators and generators to efficiently process data in our applications.

Iterables and Iterators

A lot of effort has been put into the latest release of the ECMAScript standard to improve the way we organize our code. ES6 has a whole new traversing mechanism that makes it really simple and easy to implement an iterable and an iterator. This version of JavaScript introduces a set of protocols called as Iterator and Iterable Protocols, which should be implemented by any JavaScript object to become an iterator or an iterable. Before moving ahead and discussing these protocols, let's take a look at iterables and iterators in JavaScript:

Put simply, an iterator pattern is a structured pattern for fetching information from a collection of elements, element by element, in a specific order. It is an object with a specific interface designed for iteration. This pattern has always been around and has been used in JavaScript through custom objects, but with ES6, we are introduced to an implicit standardization of the iterators pattern. Many existing data structures in JavaScript now expose an iterator, and you can also construct your own iterator using the same standard, providing you with maximum interoperability.

An **Iterable** is a simple representation of a series of elements that can be iterated over. It does not have any iteration state such as a "current element." Instead, it has one method that produces an Iterator.

An **Iterator** is the object with an iteration state. All iterator objects come with a next() method that is used to return the next object in the collection. The object returned from the next() method has two properties. Namely:

(i) value, which is the next value in the collection; and

(ii) done, which is a Boolean that signals whether the sequence has ended, that is, it is false as long as there are values in the sequence to return and only returns true when the collection has run out of values.

Each call to the next() method produces the next value in the collection. Once all the values of the collection are iterated, calling the next() method will return the value as undefined and done as true.

© Deepak Grover and Hanu Kunduru 2017
D. Grover and H. P. Kunduru, *ES6 for Humans*, DOI 10.1007/978-1-4842-2623-0_8

With all that said, let's look at how you can manually implement an iterator in ES6:

```
function myIterator(data) {
        let currentIndex = 0;
        return {
        next: () => {
const done = (currentIndex >= data.length);
const value = !done ? data[currentIndex] : undefined;
currentIndex += 1;

return {
done,
value
 };
}
};
}

const itrObj = myIterator([41, 42, 43]);
itrObj.next();  // { value: 41, done: false }
itrObj.next();  // { value: 42, done: false }

itrObj.next();  // { value: 43, done: false }
itrObj.next();  // { value: undefined, done: true }

// for all further calls
console.log(itrObj.next());    // { value: undefined, done: true }
```

In the above code snippet, the myIterator() function returns an object that has a next() method, when called each time returns the next value of the collection. After the last element, the done value of the object returned becomes true and the value returned is always undefined.

ES6 simplifies the process of implementing iterators by introducing [Symbol. iterator], which specifies the default iterator for an object. This key holds the @@iterator method, which underlies the iterable protocol that will be discussed later in this chapter. Whenever an object needs to be iterated, such as at the beginning of a for..of loop, its @@iterator method is called with no arguments. This method returns the default Iterator for the object. In ES6, @@ describes a well-known symbol. Here, @@ iterator specifies the iterator function stored at the object's key [Symbol.iterator]. Therefore, for the above example, the @@iterator method would return the next() function:

```
myIterator[Symbol.iterator] = function () {
   return {
   next: function () {}
 }
}
```

Having a symbol used as the key to hold the iterator method ensures that it will never conflict with regular object keys. Now let's look at the same example as above in ES6 with Symbol.iterator in place:

```
const arr = [41, 42, 43];
const itrObj = arr[Symbol.iterator]();
itrObj.next(); // { value: 41, done: false }
itrObj.next(); // { value: 42, done: false }
itrObj.next(); // { value: 43, done: false }
itrObj.next(); // { value: undefined, done: true }
```

When the @@iterator method at Symbol.iterator is invoked for the given array arr, it will create a new iterator. Note that a fresh iterator is created every time it is invoked. Built-in ES6 data structures that are iterables have this behavior, allowing the values to be iterated over using the next() method.

Let's take a look at primitive string values as an example,

```
const message = "Ian is an awesome student";
const itrObj = message[Symbol.iterator]();

itrObj.next();      // { value: "I", done: false }
itrObj.next();      // { value: "a", done: false }
..
```

In the above example, we are able to iterate over each character of the String message using the next() method. ES6 also allows us to iterate over the new data structures, like Map and Set collections. Let's take a look at Map as an example:

```
const permissionMap = new Map();

permissionMap.set("admin", {read: true, write: true, del: true});
permissionMap.set("student", {read: true, write: false, del: false});
permissionMap.set("faculty", {read: true, write: true, del: false});
permissionMap.set("staff", {read: true, write: false, del: true});

const permissions= permissionMap[Symbol.iterator]();

console.log(permissions.next());
// {value: ['admin', { read: true, write: true, del: true }], done: false}

console.log(permissions.next());
// {value: ['student', { read: true, write: false, del: false }], done: false}

console.log(permissions.next());
// {value: ['faculty', { read: true, write: true, del: false }], done: false}
```

```
console.log(permissions.next());
// {value: ['staff', { read: true, write: false, del: true }], done: false}

console.log(permissions.next());
// {value: undefined, done: true}
```

In the above example, we have created a map for the permissions for different user types as the key. We can simply create a new iterator by invoking the @@iterator method and iterate over the values using next(). A good thing to note here is that these collections also provide API method(s) to generate an iterator, for example, you can get the iterator of a map using the entries() method:

```
const permissionEntries = permissionMap.entries();

console.log(permissionEntries.next());
// {value: ['admin', { read: true, write: true, del: true }], done: false}

console.log(permissionEntries.next());

// {value: ['student', { read: true, write: false, del: false }], done:
false}
```

Iteration Protocols

Now that we have a basic understanding of iterators and iterables, let's talk about those protocols we briefly discussed at the beginning of this chapter. There are two iteration protocols: the iterable protocol and the iterator protocol. These protocols can be implemented by any object respecting some conventions.

Iterable Protocol

The iterable protocol allows you to customize the iteration behavior of JavaScript objects. This protocol states that all objects that are iterables must implement the @@iterator method using the [Symbol.iterator] property. This method is called whenever an object needs to be iterated. It takes no arguments and returns the default iterator, which can be used to obtain the values out of the iterable. Built-in iterables such as Array, Map, Set, etc., have a default @@iterator method, which allows us to traverse the respective collections.

Iterator Protocol

The iterator protocol defines a standard way to get a sequence of values out of an iterable object. This protocol states that an iterator object must define a next() method that takes no arguments and returns an object with two properties: done and value.

Iterator as an Iterable

If an iterator is also an iterable, it can directly be used with the for...of loop. You can make an iterator an iterable by providing it with the Symbol.iterator, which returns the iterator itself. Take a look at the following code snippet where we are making an iterable from an iterator, and then using the for...of loop to iterate over:

```
const infiniteSequenceGenerator = {
        currentNumber: 0,

        // making the "infiniteSequenceGenerator" iterator an iterable
        [Symbol.iterator]() {
                return this;
        },

        next() {
                return {
                        value: this.currentNumber++,
                        done: false
                }
        }
};

const iter = infiniteSequenceGenerator[Symbol.iterator]();

console.log(iter === infiniteSequenceGenerator);   // true

console.log(iter.next().value);   // 0
console.log(iter.next().value);   // 1
console.log(iter.next().value);   // 2
console.log(iter.next().value);   // 3

for (let item of iter) {
    if (item > 20) break;
    console.log( item );
}

// 4
// 5
// 6
// 7
// ... 20
```

In the above example, notice how we can directly use the for...of loop with an iterable, but internally it uses the next() method since we got the list of numbers starting from 4 in the for...of loop, having called the iterator four times before starting the loop using the next() method manually.

return( ) and throw( ) in Iterators

An iterator also has two additional optional methods: the return(...) and throw(...), which are not implemented on most built-in iterators, but they definitely have a lot of relevance in the context of generators, which we will be looking into later in this chapter.

There might cases where you may want the last item with {done: true, value: undefined} to have some value other than being undefined. This is where return() comes in. The return(...) method is used to send a signal to an iterator that the code using the iterator will not call for anymore values from the iterator. It could be used when the iterator has consumed all the values or when it has encountered an unusual termination, allowing it to perform a cleanup operation like killing a database connection, saving, or closing a file. If present, return(...) will be called automatically when the collection has been exhausted, or it can also be called manually as well. The return(...) method takes it as an optional argument, which is generally sent back as the value in the returned object.

throw(...) on the other hand, is used to signal the iterator about an exception or an error that might have occurred. This can be used differently by an iterator compared to the signal from return(...) method because it does not imply a complete stop like return(...) does. We will be looking into these methods more closely in the generators section.

Generators

In simple words, Generators are functions that can be paused. Prior to ES6, JavaScript only had functions that would run to completion before anything could interrupt their execution. With ES6, a different kind of function has been introduced to us through generators that do not always run to completion like functions, but they can pause and resume cycle midway through executions.

A generator is a function that allows us to create a special type of iterator, whose execution can be suspended and retained while keeping the context. A function is a generator if it contains one or more yield expressions and if it uses the function * syntax:

```
function *gen() {
        yield 42;
}
```

In this syntax, the position of the '*' is not very significant. A generator can be written in any of the following ways:

```
function *gen()  { .. }
function* gen()  { .. }
function * gen() { .. }
function*gen()   { .. }
```

Nonetheless, it is preferable to maintain consistency in style when you use a generator in your code. We will use the first format in the rest of this book.

Generator Function

A generator function is paused by executing a yield keyword in the body of the function, which can be used any number of times in the function body. You can return a value from a yield expression. Check the following example where we are yielding the value 42 from a generator:

```
function *generator () {
    yield 42;
}
```

A Generator executes just like any other function and you can pass arguments in it. The only difference being that executing a generator doesn't really run the code inside it. It simply produces an iterator that can be used to execute the code inside it.

```
function *gen() {
    yield "Hello";
    yield "from";
    yield "generator";
}
```

Now if we call this generator function, it will not be executed; instead it returns an iterator that will be used to execute the code inside it.

```
let obj = gen();
```

In the generator above, the operations in the beginning would run and then the yield statement would pause the execution of the generator until the next() method is called. The method obj.next() continues the execution of gen, until the next yield expression:

```
console.log(obj.next());    // { value: "Hello", done: false}
console.log(obj.next());    // { value: "from", done: false}
console.log(obj.next());    // { value: "generator", done: false}
console.log(obj.next());    // { value: undefined, done: true}
```

yield can be used any number of times inside a generator. It can also be a part of a loop to represent a repeated pause location. Note that yield is not just a pause point, it also sends out a value when pausing the generator.

```
function *infiniteNumbers() {
    var n = 1;
    while (true) {
        yield n++;
    }
}
```

```
var numbers = infiniteNumbers(); // returns an iterable object

console.log(numbers.next()); // { value: 1, done: false }
console.log(numbers.next()); // { value: 2, done: false }
console.log(numbers.next()); // { value: 3, done: false }
```

Each time yield is called, the yielded value becomes the next value in the sequence. A yield statement without a value provided just implies that the value is undefined.

Communicating with Generators

In the previous section, we saw how generators communicate to our code using yield statements. We can also pass a value via yield to the generator function and use those values inside the generator function when the execution resumes. Take a look at the following code snippet, for example:

```
function *calculator() {
    const num1 = yield "I am a calculator";
    const num2 = yield "I add numbers";
    console.log(`Sum is: ${num1 + num2}`);
}

const myGenerator = calculator();

console.log(myGenerator.next());
// { value: 'I am a calculator', done: false }

console.log(myGenerator.next(2));
// { value: 'I add numbers', done: false }

console.log(myGenerator.next(3));
// Sum is: 5
// { value: undefined, done: true }
```

In the above example, the first time next() was called, the generator yields the "I am a calculator" string and pauses. The second time the value from the next(2) will be assigned to num1, because inside the generator, we specified that whatever value is yielded at yield "I am a calculator" gets assigned to num1, and similarly for num2. Hence, the third time next() was called, Sum is: 5 was printed to the console and since there was no more yield statements, undefined was returned as the value.

This behavior of generators to communicate well with our code can be really helpful in cases of asynchronous programming. Generators can make your asynchronous code look synchronous. Consider another example that demonstrates how generators and asynchronous code work well together:

```
function getFlightDurations() {
        setTimeout(() => {
            flightIterator.next({
                Qatar: "39h 0m",
                Emirates: "40h 20m"
            });
        }, 1200);
}

function getFlightPrices() {
        setTimeout(function(){
            flightIterator.next({
                Qatar: "$2010",
                Emirates: "$1904"
            })
        }, 1000);
}

function *getFlights() {
        const allFlights = ["Qatar", "Emirates"];
        const flightDurations = yield getFlightDurations();
        const flightPrices = yield getFlightPrices();

        for (let flight of allFlights) {
            console.log(`New York to Auckland takes
${flightDurations[flight]} in ${flight} airlines for around
${flightPrices[flight]}`);
        }
}

const flightIterator = getFlights();

flightIterator.next();
// New York to Auckland takes 39h 0m in Qatar airlines for around $2010
// New York to Auckland takes 40h 20m in Emirates airlines for around $1904
```

In the above example, genFlights() is a generator function that returns an iterator.
On calling the next() method of the returned iterator, the generator execution gets to the
first yield statement where getFlightDurations() is invoked. getFlightDurations()
is an asynchronous function that uses setTimeout to delay the execution by 1.2s and
calls next() method on the iterator guaranteeing that flightDurations will be correctly
assigned. The same happens with flightPrices and once the next() method is called
again in getFlightPrices(), the output is logged out to the console. If we were not
using yield here, flightDurations and flightPrices would simply be assigned as
undefined since the function itself would return undefined at the time of assignment.
Having a yield statement prevents the value from being assigned until the setTimeout
function has executed. This is how generators help us write blocking code when using
asynchronous operations, making the code look more synchronous.

Completing Early

Earlier in this chapter, we discussed about the iterators having two optional methods: return(...) and throw(...), which have a lot of relevance in the context of generators. These methods end the sequence in a paused generator as soon as they are called. Take a look at the following code snippet, for example:

```
function *getFruits() {
        yield "apple";
        yield "orange";
        yield "banana";
}

const fruitIterator = getFruits();

console.log(fruitIterator.next());              // {value: 'apple', done: false}

console.log(fruitIterator.return("kiwi"));  // {value: 'kiwi', done: true}

console.log(fruitIterator.next());              // {value: undefined, done: true}
```

In the above example, return("kiwi") returns the same value "kiwi" passed as the argument and ends the sequence resulting in done to be true. This is equivalent to having a return value in the generator function, although you should always keep in mind that traversing the sequence obtained from a generator does not include the value that signals { done: true }. Check the following code snippet, for example, where we are iterating over the collection fruitIterator, which only contains the elements yielded before the return() method was invoked in the source generator:

```
function *getFruits() {
        yield "apple";
        yield "orange";
        yield "banana";
        return "kiwi";
        yield "watermelon";
}

const fruitIterator = getFruits();

for (let fruit of fruitIterator) {
        console.log(fruit);
}

// apple
// orange
// banana
```

You can also avoid the immediate sequence termination by wrapping up the code inside try-finally block ensuring that the code with the finally clause will execute in case of completion, whether early or when the yield statements are exhausted. This can be helpful in performing any cleanup or closing operations after the sequence has ended. Check the following code snippet, for example:

```
function *getFruits() {
        try {
          yield "apple";
          yield "orange";
          yield "banana";
        }

        finally {
          console.log("You must always eat a big watermelon");
          yield "watermelon";
        }
}

const fruitIterator = getFruits();

console.log(fruitIterator.next());
// { value: 'apple', done: false }

console.log(fruitIterator.return("kiwi"));
// You must always eat a big watermelon
// { value: 'watermelon', done: false }

console.log(fruitIterator.next());
// { value: 'kiwi', done: true }

console.log(fruitIterator.next());
// { value: undefined, done: true }
```

In the above example, once the expressions in the finally block have been executed, the sequence will terminate with the value as 'kiwi' and done as true, where 'kiwi' was passed as the argument in the return(...) method.

Similarly, throw(...) also stops the execution of the generator but it is never called automatically. This method can be useful in cases where you may want to warn the user about some unexpected errors, utilizing a try-catch block to enable error handling in generators. Check the following code snippet, for example:

```
function *getFruits() {
        yield "apple";
        yield "orange";
        yield "spinach";
        yield "watermelon"
}
```

```
const fruitIterator = getFruits();

for (let fruit of fruitIterator) {
        try {
            console.log(fruit);
            if (fruit === "spinach") {
                fruitIterator.throw("Vegetable Found");
            }
        }
        catch (err) {
            console.log(`Exception: ${err}`);
        }
}

// apple
// orange
// spinach
// Exception: Vegetable Found
```

Notice how "watermelon" never got yielded from the generator because throw() was called when "spinach" was returned, halting the execution of the sequence.

Summary

Iterators and Generators introduced in ES6 provide a sequential access to the values stored in a collection and also allow us to customize the way we traverse these values. ES6 also introduces a new set of protocols to define iterators and iterables known as Iteration protocols. In this chapter, we learned about defining the default iterator of an object using the unique [Symbol.iterator] property. When Symbol.iterator is provided on an object, the object is considered an iterable.

In the latter half of this chapter, we also learned about Generator functions, which are indicated by a star (*) character and one or more yield statements in their function body. They are special types of functions that can be paused and resumed midway through executions.

CHAPTER 9

■ ■ ■

Promises in ES6

JavaScript, as we know it, is single threaded by design. In browsers, it uses event handling
to manage a lot of tasks concurrently. The JavaScript Engine manages an event queue
and when an event occurs, the registered handler function is called. If you have any
experience with traditional JavaScript, then you are already well aware of the fact
that understanding asynchronous programming is a must to properly be able to use
JavaScript. The main pattern for using asynchrony is through the callback function. ES6
brings to the standard JavaScript specification a new feature *Promises* (a feature available
in some of the new and latest JS libraries and frameworks) that solves many of the
significant problems in the callbacks – the only approach to async.

Promises Overview

In cases where it is required to wait for an asynchronous operation to complete and
then perform a task, JavaScript heavily relies on callbacks, allowing the code execution
to proceed past the long-running task. You must already know that setTimeout,
XMLHttpRequest, and all browser-based asynchronous functions are callback based. While
the concept is simple and easy to understand in theory, it can lead to some really confusing
and difficult-to-follow code, especially in cases when it is needed to make a callback after
a callback (nested callbacks), which is more often termed "Callback Hell." Consider the
following code snippet, for example, where X must happen before Y must happen before Z:

```
x = getData();
y = getMoreData(x);
z = getMoreData(y);
```

Prior to ES6, you could have asynchronously fetched x and then passed it as an
argument to fetch y and similarly for z, using callbacks as follows:

```
getData(function(x){
    getMoreData(x, function(y){
        getMoreData(y, function(z){
            ...
        });
    });
});
```

D. Grover and H. P. Kunduru, *ES6 for Humans*, DOI 10.1007/978-1-4842-2623-0_9

This can get more and more complex in real-life applications where you have lots of callback functions, which can lead to a callback pyramid. These callback pyramids appear everywhere – in handling HTTP requests, database manipulation, animation, interprocess communication, and all manners of other places. Generally, codes using callback functions can become harder to follow, refactor, and test.

This is where promises come in. Promises give us a way to handle asynchronous processing in a more controlled pattern. They represent a value that can be handled at some point in the future, and offer an escape from the callback hell Promises provide a simpler alternative for executing, composing, and managing asynchronous operations in comparison to callback-based approaches. They also allow the logical flow of the code to be much easier to follow.

ES6 has native support for promises. A promise is an object that is waiting for an asynchronous operation to complete, and when that operation completes, the promise is either fulfilled or rejected. A promise object can be any of these three states:

- **fulfilled** – when the promise succeeds

- **rejected** – when the promise fails

- **pending** – when it's neither fulfilled or rejected

A pending promise may transition into a fulfilled or rejected state, and the promise is considered to be settled when it's either fulfilled or rejected. It is important to note a settled promise is immutable, which means that once a promise is settled, it cannot be resettled.

Creating a Promise

Promises are created using the new `Promise()` constructor that accepts an **executor** (a function) that takes two parameters:

- The first parameter (typically named resolve) is a function that is called with the future value when it's ready, that is, when the promise is fulfilled;

- And the second parameter (typically named reject) is a function that is called to reject the promise if it can't resolve the future value.

The **executor** initiates some asynchronous work and then, once that completes, calls either the resolve or reject function to resolve the promise or else reject it if an error occurred.

A simple Promise looks like this:

```
const p = new Promise((resolve, reject) => {
    if (/* some condition */) {
        resolve(/* some value */);  // fulfilled successfully
    } else {
        reject(/* some reason */);  // error, rejected
    }
});
```

The second method (reject) is optional, and you can very well create a promise with only the resolve method, as demonstrated in the code snippet below where the promises are fulfilled and rejected, respectively:

```
new Promise(resolve => resolve()) // promise is fulfilled
new Promise((resolve, reject) => reject()) // promise is rejected
```

You can also create an immediately resolved promise using:

```
const sayHello = Promise.resolve("hello!");
```

Similarly, you can also reject a promise using Promise.reject(value). Resolving or rejecting a promise without a value isn't very useful. Usually, a promise will resolve to some value that could be a result from an HTTP request, animation, or some other asynchronous operation.

A promise, once created, can only be settled, meaning it can either be fulfilled or rejected. And as stated above, since a settled promise is immutable, the settled value or failure reason cannot be changed (the value can be undefined as well). However, an object may be used as the fulfilled value, and object properties may mutate.

Consuming a Promise with then() and catch()

Once a promise is created, it can be passed around as a value, essentially representing a placeholder for a future value. This value can be consumed when the promise is fulfilled using .then() method. This method takes a function that will be passed to the resolved value of the Promise once it is fulfilled. Consider the following code snippet, for example:

```
const p = new Promise((resolve, reject) => resolve(42));
p.then((val) => console.log(val)); // 42
```

Every promise must have a .then() method that actually takes two possible parameters. The first parameter is the function to be called when the promise is fulfilled and the second parameter is a function to be called if the promise is rejected as depicted in Figure 9-1.

```
p.then((value) => { console.log("Promise Fulfilled:", value) },
       (error) => { console.log("Promise Rejected: ", error) });
```

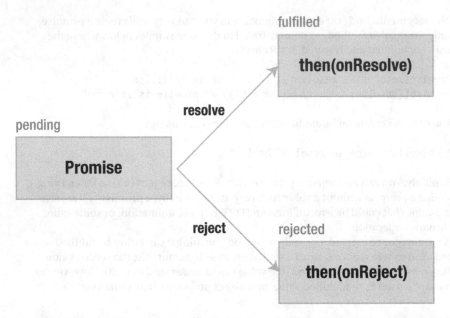

Figure 9-1. *A pending promise can be fulfilled or rejected and handled using .then() method*

If a given promise always gets resolved, we can omit the second parameter for simplicity. Check out the following example where the customer gets his pizza five seconds after the order:

```
const pizza = new Promise((resolve) => {
      console.log("Getting your pizza in 5 seconds...");
      setTimeout(() => {
            resolve("Onion Pizza");
      }, 5000);
});

pizza.then(
(item) => { console.log(`Order Received: ${item}`) },
(error) => { console.log("Something went wrong with your pizza") }
);

// Getting your pizza in 5 seconds...
// Order Received: Onion Pizza
```

This example demonstrates two things:

- First, that the handlers we attached to the promise were called after all other code ran, asynchronously.

- Second, that the fulfillment handler was called only when the promise was fulfilled, with the value it was resolved with (in our case, the onion pizza). The same holds true for the rejection handler.

Here's another typical example of consuming a promise, where getRentalList(location) is asynchronous and returns the list of currently available rental properties at the given location using a web service that returns a promise:

```
const housingPromise = getRentalList("London");
housingPromise.then(
    (res) => {
        if (res.properties && res.properties.length > 0) {
            console.log(`We found the houses for you: ${res.properties}`);
        } else {
            console.log(`Sorry, no housing is available in ${res.
            location}`);
        }
    },
    (error) => {
        console.log(`Something went wrong: ${error}`);
    }
);
```

If you're only interested in rejecting a promise, you can omit the first parameter and pass it as null. Check the following code snippet, for example:

```
const networkReq = new Promise((resolve, reject) => {
    reject("No Server Found");
});
networkReq.then(
    null,
    (error) => { console.log(error); }
);
```

On the one hand, if a handler returns a value in the a .then() call, it is automatically wrapped in a promise when returned. These .then() calls can be chained. We will get into the details of how the chaining of promises work in the next section. On the other hand, you can also handle a **rejected** promise in a more compact way using the catch() method. For instance, you can rewrite the above example as follows:

```
networkReq.catch((error) => { console.log(error); });
```

The catch() method is useful for error handling in promise composition. Similar to then() method, it also returns a promise, but only deals with the rejected cases. catch() method behaves as an abbreviation for then(null, onRejected). We will learn more about handling errors later in this chapter.

Chaining of Promises

Since .then() and .catch() always return a new promise, it is easy to chain promises with extreme control over how and where the errors are handled. Chaining promises allows asynchronous operations to be chained together, so that they are guaranteed to happen in the correct and expected order, resulting in code that looks almost synchronous. Consider the following example:

```
const bond = new Promise((resolve, reject) => {
    resolve("Bond");
});

bond.then((str) => `${str}, James ${str}`)
    .then((str) => `Hello, I'm ${str}!`)
    .then((str) => console.log(str));

// Hello, I'm Bond, James Bond!
```

Above is a simple example of how chaining promises can help in a sequential executing of different tasks and get the end result. Let's take a look at the following code snippet that is more realistic example of how chaining of promises can be beneficial with asynchronous tasks:

```
getPaymentFromUser
    .then(displayTransactionDetails)
    .then(queueTransactionEmail)
    .then(redirectToOrdersPage)
    .catch(logError)
```

Here, getPaymentFromUser returns a promise, and each function in the promise chain gets called with the return value of the previous handler once it has completed. In this example, displayTransactionDetails() will wait for getPaymentFromUser() to complete before starting, and queueTransactionEmail() will wait for displayTransactionDetails() to complete before starting, and so on. It is important to note that logError() will only run if any of the previous promises reject. This serializes the calls without blocking the main execution thread and guaranteeing that the executing of these operations will happen in the serial order.

Error Handling

Previously in this chapter, we discussed how we can handle errors while consuming promises using any of the following ways:

```
somePromise().then(onResolved, onRejected);

// or simply using catch()

somePromise()
    .then(onResolved)
    .catch(onRejected);
```

But which one should you prefer and why? The answer to this question lies in the very scenario where your onResolved() function throws an error. The promise returned from then() method will be rejected, but using the first way, the rejection cannot be caught—resulting in the error to get swallowed in your app. But using the second way, errors originating from both somePromise() and onResolved() can be handled at the catch() method. If we have more than one then() call, then the error is passed on until there is an error handler. Therefore, it is recommended to end all promise chains with a catch() method.

Combining Promises with `Promises.all`

Promise.all takes an array of promises (or any iterable) and returns a promise that resolves when all of the promises in the iterable argument have resolved, or rejects with the reason of the first passed promise that rejects.

If any of the passed in promises rejects, then all the promises immediately reject with the value of the promise that rejected, discarding all the other promises whether or not they have resolved. Note that if an empty array is passed, then this method resolves immediately.

```
const p1 = Promise.resolve(3);
const p2 = 42;
const p3 = new Promise((resolve, reject) => {
    setTimeout(resolve, 100, "foo");
});

Promise.all([p1, p2, p3]).then(values => {
    console.log(values); // [3, 42, "foo"]
});
```

However, in some cases, you may not want to wait for all the promises in your array to resolve, but simply want to get the results of the first promise in the array to fulfill. In that scenario, Promise.race() can be used.

Promise.race() also takes an array of promises, but unlike Promise.all(), it will fulfill its returned promise as soon as the first promise in that array fulfills. For example, consider the case where we want to fetch some JSON data from an API endpoint, but we don't want to wait forever for the response. In that case, we just want to use a default value instead. We can implement this using Promise.race():

```
// A Promise that times out after given time (t)
function delay(t) {
    return new Promise((resolve, reject) => {
        setTimeout(resolve, t);
    });
}
```

```
// Whichever Promise fulfills first is the result passed to our handler
Promise.race([
    fetchData(),
    delay(5000).then(() => { data: "test" })
])
.then((res) => {
    // this will be "test" if fetchData() takes longer than 5 sec.
    console.log("data:", res.data);
})
.catch(function(err) {
    console.log("error:", err);
});
```

In this example, the delay() function returns a new promise that resolves after t milliseconds. We then attach a handler to that returned promise to return our default user object {user: "guest"}, which ensures that if we get user data from our server within 5 seconds, we will get the user details; otherwise a guest user will be used.

Summary

Promises have become the standard approach for dealing with large amounts of asynchronous operations. In this chapter, we learned how promises, when used correctly, produce easy-to-read code, which makes them easier to debug than traditional callbacks. They allow us to combine asynchronous APIs and let us to wrap non-spec compliant promise APIs or callback APIs with real promises. Unlike callbacks and events, promises help us avoid race conditions and assure immutability of the value represented by it. Promises let us write asynchronous code in a synchronous fashion, with flat indentation and a single exception channel.

CHAPTER 10

■ ■ ■

Meta Programming

The term "meta" characterizes something that is characteristically self-referential. In terms of programming, meta programming means to program the programming of the program itself. It could be inspecting or modifying the structure of the program, or changing the way things work in the language itself. ES6 introduces a great set of features around meta programming, providing low-level hooks into the code mechanics of the program. In this chapter, we will dig into those features in details and see how meta programming works in JavaScript.

Meta Programming in ES5 and ES6 Overview

The concept of meta programming is not new to JavaScript. You're probably using meta programming every day without even realizing it. For example, checking whether an object is a prototype of another object, we use a.isPrototypeOf(b). This is a form of meta programming. Generally, all of the Object.* methods can be considered a form of meta programming. Meta programming provides a way to utilize the features and capabilities of the language, enabling you to make programs with greater flexibility and efficiently handle custom needs of your applications.

A key strategy of meta programming is reflection. It allows us to inspect, or modify the structure of a program, or alter the behavior of the internals (specifically metadata properties and functions) of a program at runtime. ES6 offers reflection using three forms of meta programming.

There are three forms of meta programming: *introspection, self-modification,* and *intercession.*

- **Introspection** – when you have a code inspecting itself, for example: a.isPrototypeOf(b) is introspection. typeof, instanceof are also introspection operators as they gather information about the code.

- **Self-modification** – when you modify the structure of a program. One such example would be Object.defineProperty() method, which defines a new property on an object or modifies the existing one if it exists:

© Deepak Grover and Hanu Kunduru 2017
D. Grover and H. P. Kunduru, *ES6 for Humans*, DOI 10.1007/978-1-4842-2623-0_10

```
let cake = {};

console.log(cake);       // {}

Object.defineProperty(cake, "ingredients", {
    value: ["sugar", "all things nice"],
    enumerable: true,
    configurable: true,
    writable: true
});

console.log(cake);
// { ingredients: [ 'sugar', 'all things nice' ] }
```

In the above example, notice how we modified the structure of the cake object using `Object.defineProperty()`. Self-modification deals with the ability to access or create new properties and modify the structure of a program in runtime.

- **Intercession** – when your code modifies the default behavior, resulting in affecting the rest of the code. Intercession deals with modification of semantics of the language, or adding new constructs to your program at runtime. This is new to ES6 and we will learn more about it later in this chapter.

ES6 introduces meta programming using three new APIs: Symbol, Proxy, and Reflect. Previously in this book, we have seen how symbols allow us to create unique and immutable identifiers. They offer us a way to efficiently create unique and non-enumerable properties for an object, which can be good for separating the metadata of the object from its public interface. Symbols also help us customize the default iteration behavior of an object, essentially offering Reflection (self-modification) by enabling us to modify the behavior of a program or create new (and unique) properties on an object in runtime. Now let's take a look at what Proxy and Reflect bring to the table.

Proxies in ES6

Proxies represent intercession forms of meta programming. Proxy objects allow us to intercept any program's behavior. They enable us to modify the operations of an object and implement custom behaviors. In simpler words, there are many operations that can be performed on an object, and proxies help us to modify such operations and implement desired behaviors. These operations can be property lookup, assignment, enumeration, function invocation, etc.

A proxy object wraps the target object and modifies its behavior. We can create a proxy using:

```
const proxy = new Proxy(target, handler);
```

where target is the object whose behaviors are being modified and handler is an object whose properties are functions (referred as traps), which are called when various operations are performed against the proxy. Handler objects allow us to define the new behavior of the target object. It enables us to perform extra logic in addition to forwarding the operations onto the target/wrapped object.

Traps in Proxy Handler

A handler object offers a list of methods that serve as traps for a proxy. These methods are optional and if a trap has not been defined, the default behavior is to forward the operation to the target.

Most common traps are for getters and setters. Take a look at the following code snippet, for example, where we have defined a trap for the get property accessor method:

```
const restaurant = {
    soda: 2,
    burger: 1
};

const restHandler = {
    get: function(target, property) {
        if (property in target && target[property] > 0) {
            target[property] -= 1;
            return `Enjoy your ${property}`;
        }
        return `Sorry, We are out of ${property}s!`;
    }
};

const restProxy = new Proxy(restaurant, restHandler);

console.log(restProxy.soda);
// Enjoy your soda

console.log(restProxy.soda);
// Enjoy your soda

console.log(restProxy.soda);
// Sorry, We are out of sodas!

console.log(restProxy.burger);
// Enjoy your burger

console.log(restProxy.burger);
// Sorry, We are out of burgers!
```

In the above example, we have a restaurant object that contains the list and the quantities of available inventory. We are using proxy to wrap the restaurant object, which enables us to intercept (or "trap") native operations of the restaurant object and execute the modified behavior on it. Here, the handler object contains a trap for the get property accessor that receives the target and the property name when invoked. This method traps all the "get property accessor" invocations and checks if the property exists and if its value is greater than 0, and if it does, its value is decremented and the message `Enjoy your ${property}` is returned; otherwise, the message is, `Sorry, We are out of ${property}s!` is returned. This "get" trap can be used to trap all the getter events on the target object. Similarly, you can also intercept setter events. Check the following code snippet, for example:

```
const restaurant = {
    soda: 5
};
const restHandler = {
    set: function(target, property, value) {
        target[property] = value;
        console.log(`${property} has been added to inventory`);
    }
}

const restProxy = new Proxy(restaurant, restHandler);

restProxy.beer = 10;
// beer has been added to inventory
```

In this example, we overwrite the set property accessor method, which overrides the default assignment. Proxies can be extremely useful when it comes to validation. We can easily validate the passed value for an object using set handler. For example, let's suppose that we are creating a voting application and only people above 18 years of age and having residency of the country are allowed to vote:

```
const voterValidator = {
    set: function(obj, prop, value) {
        if (prop === "age") {
            if (!Number.isInteger(value)) {
                throw new TypeError("Input age is not an integer");
            }
            if (value < 18) {
                throw new RangeError("Input age seems invalid");
            }
        } else if (prop === "residency") {
            if (value === false) {
                throw new Error("Residency is mandatory to vote");
            }
        }
```

```
    // The default behavior to store the value
    obj[prop] = value;

    // Indicate success
    return true;
  }
};

const person = new Proxy({}, voterValidator);

person.age = 23;
person.residency = false;    // Throws an exception
person.age = "young";        // Throws an exception
person.age = 200;            // Throws an exception
```

Another good use case for set trap would be data-binding, where you can have a callback method in place, which will be invoked when a property is set and that callback method can react to the changes made to the target object's property.

Besides **setters** and **getters**, proxy offers a range of other traps that you can set up. Below are some of those traps that can help you understand proxy better.

has

has is used to trap "in" operator. has can be incredibly useful if you want to hide a particular property of an object. We can return false even if the property is present on an object. Check out the following example where we are hiding beer inventory from the restaurant object using the has method to trap "in" operator.

```
const restaurant = {
    soda: 5,
    beer: 10
};
const restHandler = {
    has: function(target, property) {
        if (property === "beer") {
            return false;
        }
        return property in target;
    }
}

const restProxy = new Proxy(restaurant, restHandler);
console.log("beer" in restProxy);    // false
console.log("soda" in restProxy);    // true
```

In the above example, all "in" operator invocations are trapped in the "has" method and if the property name is "beer," false is returned; otherwise the default behavior is maintained (check property in target). Note that a "has" can only help you in preventing the detection of a particular property from "in" operator. The property is still enumerable and can be accessed via a for...in loop.

ownKeys

ownKeys is used to trap the access of the owned properties and owned symbol properties via Object.keys(), Object.getOwnPropertyNames() or Object.getOwnSymbolProperties(). This can also be used in combination with the has trap handler to strengthen the privacy of the target object properties. (Note that these properties would still not be completely private):

```
const restaurant = {
    soda: 5,
    beer: 10
};

const restHandler = {
    has: function(target, property) {
        if (property === "beer") {
            return false;
        }
        return property in target;
    },

    ownKeys: function(target) {
        return ["soda"];
    }
}

const restProxy = new Proxy(restaurant, restHandler);

console.log("beer" in restProxy);           // false
console.log(Object.keys(restProxy));        // ["soda"]
```

You can also add another trap handler: getOwnPropertyDescriptor, which traps the Object.getOwnPropertyDescriptor() calls, to enhance the privacy.

apply

apply is used to trap a function invocation. It takes three arguments:

- **target**: the target function whose behavior is being modified;
- **context**: the context passed as this to target on invocation;
- **args**: the arguments passed when applying the call.

Take a look at the following code snippet, for example, where we are applying a season discount on the final billing amount using the apply trap handler:

```
function getBill(amount) {
    return amount;
}

const billHandler = {
    apply: function(target, context, args) {
        console.log("Applying Discount of 35%");
        return args[0] - (args[0] * 0.35);
    }
}

const billProxy = new Proxy(getBill, billHandler);

console.log(billProxy(300));
// Applying Discount of 35%
// 195
```

Since the target object here is a function, these are also called as function traps, and you can alternatively have traps for .call() and .bind() methods also

Up until this point, we have covered enough trap handlers to give you an overall picture. We have seen how Proxy helps us intercepting setters and getters, decorating objects, adding validation rules, enhancing privacy, and essentially modifying the default behavior of an object. You can explore through more trap handlers at the following link: - https://developer.mozilla.org/en-US/docs/Web/JavaScript/Guide/Meta_programming.

Revocable Proxy

ES6 allows us to create proxies that can be revoked. Proxy.revocable() method is used to create a revocable proxy object. Similar to a proxy object, it also takes a handler and a target object and returns a newly created revocable proxy object.

A revocable proxy object has two properties: proxy and revoke.

```
const { proxy, revoke } = Proxy.revocable(target, handler);
```

where,

- **proxy** – A Proxy object created with new Proxy (target, handler) call
- **revoke** – A function with no argument to invalidate (switch off) the proxy.

If the revoke() function gets called, the proxy becomes unusable, which means any trap to a handler will throw a TypeError. Once a proxy is revoked, it will remain revoked and can be garbage collected. Subsequent calls of revoke have no further effect. Check the following code snippet, for example:

```
const restaurant = {
    soda: 10,
    beer: 5
};

const { proxy, revoke } = Proxy.revocable(restaurant, {});

console.log(proxy.soda);    // 10
console.log(proxy.beer);    // 5

revoke();

console.log(proxy.soda);    // TypeError: Revoked
```

Since Revocable Proxy allows you to completely cut off the Proxy and its traps, it can be useful in cases to enhance the security of an object where if attempts to access a private property has been made, the proxy can be revoked. We can modify the above example to enhance the privacy of beer property as follows:

```
const restaurant = {
    soda: 10,
    beer: 5
};

const resthandler = {
    get: function(target, property) {
        if (property === "beer") {
            revoke();
            return undefined;
        }
        return target[property];
    }
}
const { proxy, revoke } = Proxy.revocable(restaurant, resthandler);

console.log(proxy.soda);    // 10
console.log(proxy.beer);    // undefined
console.log(proxy.soda);    // TypeError: Revoked
```

In the above example, we are returning undefined and revoking the proxy if beer property is accessed, cutting off further calls to the target object via proxy.

Up until this point, we have seen how self-modification and intercession works in ES6. Now, let's take a look at Reflection through introspection.

Reflect

Reflect is a built-in global object that provides a range of introspection methods. These methods essentially gather information about the runtime-level meta-operations on objects. Besides already existing introspection methods like typeof, instanceof, etc., Reflect serves as a single object wrapper for a collection of many significant internal methods that are available exclusively through the JavaScript engine internals. A simple implementation of Reflect would look like this:

```
const restaurant = {
    soda: 10,
    beer: 5
};

console.log(Reflect.ownKeys(restaurant));
// ["soda", "beer"]
```

Note that Reflect is a static object and therefore cannot be used with the new keyword.

For every trap method in ES6 Proxy, there is a matching reflection method available in Reflect. Therefore, Reflect is also useful for implementing traps in proxies. Check the following code snippet where we are using Reflect with Proxy:

```
const restaurant = {
    soda: 2,
    beer: 5
};

const restHandler = {
    get: function(target, property) {
        if (property === "beer") {
            return undefined;
        }
        return Reflect.get(target, property);
    }
};

const restProxy = new Proxy(restaurant, restHandler);

console.log(restProxy.beer);
// undefined

console.log(restProxy.soda);
// 2
```

Again, in the above example, we are preventing the access to beer and using Reflect.get() to access other properties of the target object. One of the reasons why you should prefer using Reflect over the traditional target[property] way is this: if Reflect.get is used on a non-object target, it will throw an error, whereas target[property] would simply return undefined. Therefore, it is a good practice to use Reflect.get here. Check the following code snippet, for example, where we are trying to get a property on a non-object target:

```
console.log(Reflect.get(1, "name"));
// TypeError: Reflect.get called on non-object

console.log(1["name"]);
// undefined
```

Besides this, it is also recommended to use Reflect when calling methods on Function.prototype, because if the arguments list is null or undefined, Function.prototype.apply will call the function with no arguments, whereas Reflect.apply will throw an error. Another reason is that Reflect offers a shorter syntax, whereas Function.prototype looks much too verbose. Take a look at the following code snippet, for example:

```
function sayHello() {
    console.log(`${this.name} says hello`);
}

const person = {
    name: "Jack"
};

Function.prototype.apply.call(sayHello, person);
// Jack says hello

Reflect.apply(sayHello, person);
// TypeError: CreateListFromArrayLike called on non-object

Reflect.apply(sayHello, person, []);
// Jack says hello
```

Similarly, there are many other useful static functions, some of which have the same names as the proxy handler methods, and here are some common ones that can be helpful:

- **Reflect.get()** – A function that returns the value of properties.

- **Reflect.set()** – A function that assigns values to properties. Returns a Boolean that is true if the update was successful.

- **Reflect.getPrototypeOf()** – Same as Object.getPrototypeOf().

- **Reflect.has()** – The in operator as function. Returns a Boolean indicating whether an own or inherited property exists.

Summary

Meta Programming in ES6 offers us a way to modify the behavior of the internal language features by providing us low-level hooks into the code mechanics of the program. It comes in three forms: introspection, self-modification, and intercession.

In this chapter, we learned about the new Proxy and Reflect API, which help us with implementing different forms of meta programming. We also looked at some interesting examples where Proxy helped us with managing private properties in an object. We learned about various trap handler methods that come with Proxy, and their one-to-one mapped static Reflect methods and how we can use them in our applications to our advantage. As future ECMAScript versions are shaping up, we expect to see more interesting meta programming features that will allow us to play around with the default internal operations of the language more extensively.

CHAPTER 11

■ ■ ■

Beyond ES6

As already described in the first chapter, the ES6 release is very big, and it is a significant update to the existing versions of JavaScript, namely ES5. We have gone over all the major changes extensively in the previous chapters of this book. It took more than six years for TC39 to come up with a new version of the language and involved introducing a lot of radically new concepts and functionalities into the language. One of the major decisions taken by the committee toward the end of the release was that they would not wait too long before coming to a conclusion and releasing new features as it was done previously. They decided to officially name ES6 as ES2015 and going forward, smaller incremental updates would be released for the language and it would be denoted by the year of release. In this chapter, we will be looking at the changes and newer features that are a part of ES2016 and ES2017.

ES2016

ES2016 is a small incremental update to the existing ES2015 (ES6) release with the introduction of the Array.prototype.includes and the Exponentiation operator (**). You can also check the KangaX compatibility table to see how well the new features of ES2016 are supported on different browsers and platforms that support JavaScript: https://kangax.github.io/compat-table/es2016plus/.

The includes method on Arrays

ES2016 introduces the includes method to the Array prototype in JavaScript. You can check if an element exists in an Array using this method. It will return a Boolean value based on whether or not the element passed to it is a part of the array it is used on. Consider the following example:

```
['apple', 'banana', 'carrot'].includes('apple');   //true
['apple', 'banana', 'carrot'].includes('orange');  //false
```

© Deepak Grover and Hanu Kunduru 2017

D. Grover and H. P. Kunduru, *ES6 for Humans*, DOI 10.1007/978-1-4842-2623-0_11

As you can see in the above example, using the includes method on an array of fruits returns true if the element passed to it is a part of the array, otherwise it returns false. This check traditionally in JavaScript was done using the indexOf method, which returns the index of the number if present, otherwise -1. So basically the above example is equivalent to:

```
['apple', 'banana', 'carrot'].indexOf('apple') >= 0;    //true
['apple', 'banana', 'carrot'].indexOf('orange') >= 0;   //false
```

The above two statements work exactly like the previous example using includes, but the major difference between includes() and indexOf() is the way they interact with the value NaN (Not a Number), which helps in identifying the value.

```
const arr = [NaN];
arr.includes(NaN);              // true
arr.indexOf(NaN);              // -1
```

From this example, it is apparent that indexOf cannot be used to check for NaN values inside an array, but the includes method allows us to check if a NaN value exists inside an array.

The Exponentiation Operator **

The exponentiation operator is a new arithmetic operator introduced in ES2016 that is very much like its counterpart in languages like Python, where a double asterisk is used to calculate the exponent value of a number. It is equivalent to the traditional pow() function of the Math library.

```
let a = 2;
let b = 3;
a ** b                  //8
Math.pow(a, b)          // 8
```

Using the exponentiation Operator is a quick way to calculate the value when a number is raised to the corresponding power like in this case 2 raised to the power of 3 is 8.

ES2017

ES2017 brings in two major new features to the language, namely, Async functions and atomics with Shared memory. It also includes other simpler features like Object.entries(), Object.values(), Object.getOwnPropertyDescriptors(), padStart, padEnd, and the ability to use trailing commas in function parameter lists and calls. Let us look at each of them in greater detail.

Asynchronous Functions

ES2017 introduces an exciting new way of dealing with asynchronous code, which is the way of life in JavaScript. We have already been introduced to a popular way of handling asynchronous operations with promises. ES2017 further builds on this pattern by making it work in an synchronous manner using async and await keywords. To understand this properly, consider the following example, where we are simply creating a function that returns a promise:

```
function getData(site) {
  return fetch(site)
    .then(request => request.json())
}
```

For the above example, invoking the getData() function would return a promise, which will get settled in the context of our execution asynchronously. Now using the async / await keyword, we can have the above promise-based approach to take advantage of the generator pattern and make our code behave synchronously. async always returns a promise, which can be resolved to a value and await suspends the execution until the promise is settled. We can rewrite the above example with the async/await keywords as follows:

```
async function getData(site) {
    let request = await fetch(url);
    let text = await request.text();
    return JSON.parse(text);
}
```

Note that the await keyword works with promises only, and casts the expression into a promise if it's not one. You can also use async in function expressions, method definitions, and arrow functions like the following examples:

```
// Using function expression:
const getData = async function () {};
```

```
// Using method definition:
const item = { async getData() {} }
```

```
// Using arrow function:
const item = async () => {};
```

You might be curious about the await keyword used in the previous example: the await operator waits for the operand, that is, the promise to be settled and if the promised is fulfilled, its result is the fulfillment value and if the promise is rejected, it throws the rejection value. Therefore, we can use a traditional try catch block with async/ await to handle the promises in a better way.

Atomics and Shared Memory

Anyone used to WebWorkers will already be aware of the process of creating workers. They are created by allocating Worker objects and passing into them the script that needs to be run. The worker communicates over a message channel, and many types of data can be sent through this channel, and the type and structure is preserved when it arrives at the destination. In ES2017, to allocate shared memory you can simply use the SharedArrayBuffer constructor. It is just like a normal ArrayBuffer but its memory is shared.

Also, this new spec in ES2017 brings to us the concept of new low-level Atomics namespace object, which along with the SharedArrayBuffer constructor, provides us with primitive buildings blocks for higher-level concurrency abstractions. You can use these features to share data from a SharedArrayBuffer object among several web workers and the core thread. This lets you be able to profit from being able to easily share data among workers, giving you better coordination among them. A more detailed tutorial and specification on this topic written by Lars Hansen, the original proposal writer for Shared Memory and Atomics can be found online at the following link: - https://github.com/tc39/ecmascript_sharedmem/blob/master/TUTORIAL.md, but it is outside the scope of this book.

Object.entries() and Object.values()

Object.entries() and Object.values() are two new methods introduced in ES2017. The Object.entries() method, when run on an object, returns the object's own enumerable property [key, value] pairs in the same order as that provided by a for-in loop. But unlike the for-in loop it does not enumerate properties in the prototype chain. Similarly the Object.values() when passed an object returns an array of its own enumerable property values:

```
const myObj = { a: 1, b: 42 };

Object.entries(myObj);      // [['a', 1], ['b', 42]]

Object.values(myObj);       // [1, 42]
```

As you can see in the above example, when the Object.entries() method is passed, the object returns an array with its key/value pairs, while Object.values() method returns the property values.

padStart and padEnd

The padStart() and padEnd() method are two new string methods introduced in ES2017 that help in adding padding to a string so that the resulting string is of the length passed into them as the first parameter. You can also pass in a second optional parameter of another string you can use to pad instead of the default space. Consider the following examples:

```
'string'.padStart(10);            // "    string"

'string'.padStart(10, "abc");     // "abcastring"

'string'.padStart(10,"123465");   // "1234string"
```

```
'string'.padStart(8, "0");        // "00string"

'string'.padStart(3);             // "string"

'string'.padEnd(10);              // "string    "

'string'.padEnd(10, "abc");       // "stringabca"

'string'.padEnd(8, "123456");     // "string12"

'string'.padEnd(1);               // "string"
```

As you can see in the examples above, the add padding to the giving string makes it so that the resulting string length is either greater than the length of the first parameter based on how long its original is; if the given length is greater, the adequate amount of padding is added to the string at the start or the end based on which method you use. You can also use a second parameter to use a different string to pad instead of spaces.

Object.getOwnPropertyDescriptors()

As the name suggests, the Object.getOwnPropertyDescriptors() is a new method in ES2017 that lets you precisely examine the description of all the own properties of the given object. The property in a JavaScript object usually consists of a name that is a string and a property descriptor. The descriptor is a record of the property *value*, Boolean *writable*, a *get* function, a *set* function, a Boolean *configurable*, and a Boolean *enumerable*. Consider the following example:

```
const myObj = {
    [Symbol('mySymbol')]: 42,
    get random() { return 'test' },
};

console.log(Object.getOwnPropertyDescriptors(myObj));

// Object {random: Object, Symbol(mySymbol): Object}

// {random:{
//     configurable: true,
//     enumerable: true,
//     get: function random(),
//     set: undefined}
//[Symbol('mySymbol')]:{
//     configurable: true,
//     enumerable: true,
//     value: 42,
//     writable: true}
//}
```

The output of using the `Object.getOwnPropertyDescriptors()` on an object like `myObj` will more or less be like above. Note that all of the above features are fairly new and experimental so you might not always get the exact same results. That being said, they are becoming more and more standard now.

Trailing Commas in Function Parameter lists & calls

This feature in ES2017 is a simple syntax update. Prior to introducing this feature, having a comma after the last function parameter was not allowed in JavaScript even though the rest of the spec had this fairly commonly as in the case of Arrays and Object Literals. With this update in ES2017, you have a more uniform trailing commas syntax across JavaScript. So you can do something like this,

```
const trailFunct = function(x, y, z,) {
    //function body
}
```

This is purely a syntax update to the language and has no significant change on the behavior or functionalities in the language.

Summary

In this chapter, we looked at the various small and incremental changes to JavaScript and updates on top of ES6 that have currently been released at the time of writing this book. TC39 aims to have an annual release of new specifications that go from a proposal phase to final spec phase and then incorporated into the language. They should be small feature updates, unlike the massive change that was ES6 (ES2015).

Index

Get the eBook for only $5!

Why limit yourself?

With most of our titles available in both PDF and ePUB format, you can access your content wherever and however you wish—on your PC, phone, tablet, or reader.

Since you've purchased this print book, we are happy to offer you the eBook for just $5.

To learn more, go to http://www.apress.com/companion or contact support@apress.com.

Apress®

Printed in the United States
By Bookmasters